HARCOURT

Math

Problem Solving and Reading Strategies Workbook

TEACHER EDITION
Grade 4

Harcourt

Orlando   Austin   Chicago   New York   Toronto   London   San Diego

Visit *The Learning Site!*
www.harcourtschool.com

ISBN 0-15-336533-1

5 6 7 8 9 10   054   10 09 08 07 06 05

CONTENTS

Understand Place Value

Write the correct answer.

1. Write seventy thousand, two hundred four in standard form.

   _____ 70,204 _____

2. Write the number 55,095 in expanded form.

   _____ 50,000 + 5,000 + 90 + 5 _____

3. Nina spent $8.50 for movie tickets, $3.25 for popcorn, and $1.25 for a drink. How much did Nina spend in all?

   _____ $13.00 _____

4. Write the number that is 1,000 more than sixty-five thousand, four hundred ninety-one.

   _____ 66,491 _____

Choose the letter of the correct answer.

5. What is the word form for the number 8,407?

   A eight thousand, seventy
   B eight thousand, forty-seven
   C eight hundred forty-seven
   D eight thousand, four hundred seven

6. What is the standard form for 20,000 + 2,000 + 200 + 2?

   F 22,220
   G 22,202
   H 22,022
   J 22,002

7. Light from the sun takes about 8 minutes to get to Earth. Pam sees the sun peek out from behind a cloud at 10:52 A.M. At what time did the sunlight leave the sun?

   A About 2:52 A.M.
   B About 10:44 A.M.
   C About 10:46 A.M.
   D About 10:54 A.M.

8. Samantha deposits two checks at her bank. One check reads "five thousand, seven dollars." The other check reads "four hundred thirty-one dollars." Which number shows the total amount Samantha deposits?

   F $5,431
   G $5,437
   H $5,438
   J $5,439

9. **Write About It** Explain how you solved Problem 8.

   Possible answer: I wrote both numbers in standard form, and then I

   added the digits in each place value to find the total.

Place Value Through Hundred Thousands

Write the correct answer.

1. If 485,938 is increased by 10,000, what is the new number in standard form?

_____ 495,938 _____

2. If 762,485 is decreased by 100,000, what is the new number in standard form?

_____ 662,485 _____

3. What number am I? I have 2 digits which have a sum of 7. Both of my digits are less than 5. My tens digit is greater than my ones digit.

_____ 43 _____

4. John went to 72 baseball games during the summer and Mary went to 27 baseball games. How many more games did John see?

_____ 45 more games _____

Choose the letter of the correct answer.

5. Which number is four hundred forty thousand, seven hundred two?

A 44,000,702

B 440,702

C 44,702

D 44,072

6. What is the value of 8 in 780,762?

F 800

G 8,000

H 80,000

J 800,000

7. In a 3-digit number, the least place-value digit is 7. The greatest place-value digit is 9. Which number can it be?

A 979

B 972

C 907

D 729

8. Billy lives 2,345 miles from his grandma who lives 1,640 miles from his uncle. How far will Billy travel if he visits both?

F 3,595 miles

G 3,854 miles

H 3,985 miles

J 3,995 miles

Name _____

Place Value Through Millions

Understand → Plan → Solve → Check

Write the correct answer.

1. There were 4,542,328 visitors at the park. What is this number in expanded form?

   4,000,000 + 500,000 + 40,000

   + 2,000 + 300 + 20 + 8

2. A famous painting costs $6,780,402. What is this number in word form?

   Six million, seven hundred

   eighty thousand, four hundred
   two

3. Joe bought three tickets. Each ticket was $12.00. How much did he spend on tickets?

   $36.00

4. There were 450 books at the school book sale. There were 156 books sold. How many books are left?

   294 books

Choose the correct answer.

5. What is the standard form for the number four million, two hundred forty-eight thousand, eight hundred six?

   A 400,248,806   C 4,248,860
   B 40,248,860   D 4,248,806

6. What is the value of the 6 in 6,453,789?

   F 6 hundred
   G 6 thousand
   H 6 hundred thousand
   J 6 million

7. It takes Robert ten minutes to get from school to home. If Robert left school and arrived home at 3:00, at what time did he leave school?

   A 2:50   C 3:10
   B 2:55   D 3:15

8. Jack purchased a hat that cost $2.50. He gave the clerk the change in his pocket: 7 quarters, 6 dimes, and 4 nickels. How much change will he get?

   F 1 quarter   H 5 cents
   G 1 dime   J 3 cents

9. **Write About It** Explain your answer to Problem 8.

   Possible answer: The value of 7 quarters is 7 × $0.25 = $1.75; The value

   of 6 dimes is 6 × $0.10 = $0.60 and the value of 4 nickels is 4 × $0.05 =

   $0.20. When you add $1.75 + $0.60 + $0.20, it equals $2.55. So he gets
   $0.05 in change.

Name _____

Benchmark Numbers

Understand ➡ Plan ➡ Solve ➡ Check

Write the correct answer.

1. Write an estimate of the number of coins in pile B.

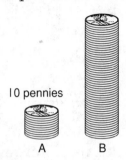

10 pennies

A   B

Possible answer: about 50 coins

2. Write an estimate of the number of peanuts in the jar.

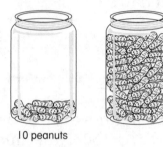

10 peanuts

Possible answer: about 50 peanuts

3. Ned buys a used car for $2,860. He must write the amount in words on his check. Write the word form for this number.

two thousand, eight hundred sixty

4. There were 360 people at the fair on Sunday and 165 people at the fair on Monday. How many people went to the fair Sunday and Monday?

525 people

Choose the letter of the correct answer.

5. Each snowball in a snowman is exactly one half as wide as the snowball below it. The snowman is made from 4 snowballs. The top snowball is 6 inches wide. How wide is the bottom snowball?

A 12 in.   C 48 in.
B 24 in.   D 96 in.

6. Harry kicked a soccer ball 3 yards farther than Jim. Jim kicked his ball 1 yard less than 20 yards. How far did Harry kick his ball?

F 21 yd   H 23 yd
G 22 yd   J 24 yd

7. **Write About It** Explain the strategy you used to solve Problem 5.

Possible answer: I made a table and wrote down the size of each snowball

by multiplying the top snowball width by 2, then multiplying that product

by 2, and so on.

© Harcourt

Summarize

Understand ➡ Plan ➡ Solve ➡ Check

Using a graph to display information is a good way to summarize data. Read the following problem.

VOCABULARY

summarize

Sue presented this data to her classmates.

NUMBER OF PETS OWNED			
Dogs	**Cats**	**Parakeets**	**Reptiles**
60,000,000	70,000,000	30,000,000	5,000,000

The class wanted to know which type of pet is owned by the most people.

---

1. Complete the graph to summarize the data in the table.

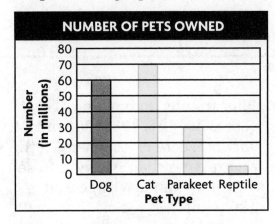

2. Solve the problem. The tallest bar indicates that there are more cats owned than dogs, parakeets, or reptiles.

3. Describe the strategy you used. Possible answer: I summarized the information in a bar graph.

4. Make a bar graph to summarize. Check students' graphs.

WEEKLY WORK SCHEDULE AT SCHOOL LIBRARY				
Student	Alice	Ralph	Trixie	Ed
Hours Worked	4	6	8	5

Name _____

Compare Numbers

Write the correct answer.

Understand ➡ Plan ➡ Solve ➡ Check

1. Write the greatest place-value position in which the digits of the two numbers are different in 385,844 and 385,855.

_____ tens _____

2. Compare the numbers 111,287 and 111,197. Write the comparison, using <, >, or =.

111,287 > 111,197 or
111,197 < 111,287

3. There were 56,731 people who visited the King Tut exhibit in May and 56,371 people who visited the exhibit in June. Which month had more visitors?

_____ May _____

4. Mike got three checks for painting houses. He wrote this expression to add the three values: $4,000 + $800 + $90. Write the total in word form.

_____ four thousand, eight hundred _____

_____ ninety dollars _____

Choose the letter of the correct answer.

5. The heaviest grizzly bear weighs 1,720 pounds. The heaviest moose weighs 1,312 pounds. The heaviest Arabian camel weighs 1,323 pounds. Which statement is true?

A The grizzly bear weighs less than the moose.

B The moose weighs more than the Arabian camel.

C The Arabian camel weighs more than the moose.

D The Arabian camel weighs more than the grizzly bear.

6. Four friends go bowling. Their scores are 126, 128, 136, and 149. Jacob's score is less than Martin's and greater than Becky's. Elise wins the game. Who scored 136 points?

F Martin

G Elise

H Jacob

J Becky

7. Write About It Explain why you made the choice you did in Problem 5.

I compared the weights of the animals in each statement by comparing

the digits in each place-value position. I started from the left to find the

larger number. Then I checked the answer choices to find the true

statement.

© Harcourt

Order Numbers

Write the correct answer.

1. Write the numbers in order from greatest to least.

    3,340; 3,675; 3,430

    3,675; 3,430; 3,340

2. Write the numbers in order from least to greatest.

    843,956; 848,965; 846,696

    843,956; 846,696; 848,965

3. Brittany threw the javelin 119 ft in Tuesday's meet. In Friday's meet, she threw the javelin 115 ft. During which meet did she throw it farther?

    Tuesday's meet

4. Caleb has three word-processing files on a diskette. The first file is 8,800 bytes. The second file is 6,500 bytes. The third file is 7,250 bytes. Write the numbers in order from greatest to least.

    8,800; 7,250; 6,500

Choose the letter of the correct answer.

5. Which line shows the numbers ordered from *least* to *greatest*?

    A 63,248; 63,284; 63,824
    B 24,824; 24,284; 24,248
    C 17,824; 17,248; 17,284
    D 9,284; 9,248; 9,824

6. Which line shows the numbers ordered from *greatest* to *least*?

    F 45,092; 45,902; 45,029; 45,920
    G 37,902; 37,920; 37,092; 37,029
    H 26,029; 26,092; 26,902; 26,920
    J 12,920; 12,902; 12,092; 12,029

7. Kate is 3 years older than Heidi. Their ages added together are 21 years. How old is each girl?

    A Kate: 18 yr; Heidi: 15 yr
    B Kate: 13 yr; Heidi: 10 yr
    C Kate: 12 yr; Heidi: 9 yr
    D Kate: 11 yr; Heidi: 10 yr

8. **Write About It** Explain the method you used to order the numbers in Problem 6.

    Possible answer: I lined up the

    numbers in their place-value

    positions and compared the

    digits. I used the hundreds

    place and the tens place to

    order the numbers.

Use Graphic Aids

Understand ▶ Plan ▶ Solve ▶ Check

Graphic aids such as tables, maps or diagrams help you solve problems. One way to organize information is to make a table.

Read the following problem.

Juan lives in Mexico in the city of León, which has a population of 1,042,132. Rosa lives in Culiacán, which has a population of 696,262. Juan's brother, Pedro, lives in Guadalajara, which has a population of 1,633,262. Jorge lives in Monterrey, which has a population of 1,088,143. Juan's uncle, who lives in Puebla, wants to see where his city of 1,222,569 stands in order of population. Can you help him?

1. Complete the table to help you solve the problem.
   Check students' work.

City	Population

2. Solve the problem.

   Possible answer: Puebla is between Guadalajara and Monterrey

   in population.

3. Describe the strategy you used.

   Possible answer: I put the cities in order from largest to smallest

   and looked for Puebla.

4. Which cities have a smaller population than Puebla?

   Monterrey, León, and Culiacán

5. Which city has a population of about two million?

   Guadalajara

PS8 Reading Strategy

© Harcourt

Name _____

Round Numbers

Write the correct answer.

Understand ➡ Plan ➡ Solve ➡ Check

1. Mercury is the speediest planet in the solar system. It orbits the Sun at an average rate of 107,030 miles per hour. Round this number to the nearest ten thousand.

_____110,000_____

2. The ballpark recorded the attendance at the opening game as 48,376. Round this number to the nearest ten thousand.

_____50,000_____

3. Describe the set of numbers which will round to 716,000 when you round to the nearest thousand.

_____all numbers from_____

_____715,500 to 716,499_____

4. Light travels about 186,000 miles in one second. Which digit is in the ten-thousands place?

_____8_____

Choose the letter of the correct answer.

5. What is the value of the underlined digit? 352,4<u>4</u>8

  A 4
  B 40
  C 400
  D 4,000

6. What is the standard form for 400,000 + 3,000 + 600 + 3?

  F 40,363
  G 43,603
  H 400,363
  J 403,603

7. Willy collected 3,542 pop tops from aluminum cans. Round this number to the nearest thousand.

  A 3,000
  B 3,500
  C 4,000
  D 4,500

8. The surface of the Earth covers 196,949,970 square miles. Round this number to the nearest million.

  F 196,000,000
  G 196,900,000
  H 197,000,000
  J 197,500,000

9. Write About It Explain how you chose your answer to Problem 8.

Possible answer: I looked at the hundred thousands place.

Since 9 > 5, the number in the millions place is increased by 1.

© Harcourt

Use Mental Math Strategies

Understand → Plan → Solve → Check

Write the correct answer.

1. Find the difference between 52 and 46.

    _____ 6 _____

2. How much greater is 95 than 86?

    _____ 9 _____

3. Danielle weighs 43 pounds and Lydia weighs 52 pounds. How much will the scale show if they both stand on it together?

    _____ 95 pounds _____

4. Ashley has saved 58 stickers and her grandmother gives her 24 more. How many does she have now?

    _____ 82 stickers _____

Choose the letter of the correct answer.

5. Which mental math problem has a sum of 8,400?

    A 3,200 + 5,200
    B 2,100 + 5,300
    C 2,400 + 5,100
    D 4,100 + 4,100

6. Marchand has saved $6.00. Which items can he buy?

    Ball $2.49   Kite $3.99
    Frisbee $2.00   Book $3.95

    F a kite and a book
    G a book and a frisbee
    H a ball and a kite
    J a book and a ball

7. Which shows the amounts in order from *greatest* to *least*?

    A $38.70; $46.72; $64.50
    B $54.70; $54.35; $54.28
    C $68.50; $68.79; $64.30
    D $74.34; $17.80; $21.56

8. Which number rounds to 140,000?

    F 114,637
    G 134,862
    H 137,428
    J 146,951

9. **Write About It** Explain how you solved Problem 6.

    Possible answer: I added the prices of the pairs of items.

Name _____

Estimate Sums and Differences

Understand ➡ Plan ➡ Solve ➡ Check

Write the correct answer.

1. Round 24,879 to the nearest *thousand*.

25,000

2. Estimate the difference using front-end estimation.

$$4,739 - 3,267$$

1,000

3. A dolphin at the Dolphin Research Center ate about 720 pounds of silverside, 990 pounds of capelin, and 950 pounds of herring in three months. About how many pounds of fish did the dolphin eat in all?

Possible answer: about 2,700 pounds

4. About 875 people passed through a toll booth on Wednesday, 732 people on Thursday, and 901 people on Friday. Use front-end estimation to estimate about how many people passed through this toll booth in all.

about 2,400 people

Choose the letter of the correct answer.

5. At two years old, a child is about one-half as tall as he or she will be as an adult. Bobbie is two years old and is 34 inches tall. About how tall will she probably be as an adult?

A About 34 in.   **C** About 78 in.
B About 68 in.   **D** About 80 in.

6. Ted is playing a game on a checkerboard. He moves his piece forward 4 squares, left 3 squares, backward 2 squares, and right 3 squares. How many squares does he have to move to be back where he started?

F 0   **H** 2
G 1   **J** 3

7. Which number is the most reasonable estimate of the sum?

$$136 + 785 + 205$$

A 1,400   **C** 1,000
B 1,100   **D** 900

8. Which number rounds to 70,000 when it is rounded to the greatest place value?

F 59,960   **H** 76,999
G 68,235   **J** 78,354

9. Write About It Describe the method you used to solve Problem 6.

Possible answer: I drew a picture of a checkerboard and marked off

each move.

Add and Subtract to 4-Digit Numbers

Write the correct answer.

1. Jon has 4,326 baseball cards and Antoine has 5,639 baseball cards. If they combine their collections, would they have more or less than Steven's collection of 9,845 cards?

_____ more _____

2. The Miller family drove 2,578 miles during their long vacation. The Brown family went across the country and traveled 5,429 miles. How much farther did the Browns travel?

_____ 2,851 miles _____

3. Mr. Smith saved $3,228 and purchased a motorcycle for $2,988. How much did he have left for his helmet?

_____ $240 _____

4. Zelda buys four items that cost $3.89, $4.59, $6.89, and $3.99. Will her $20.00 bill be enough to pay for all four items?

_____ yes _____

Choose the letter of the correct answer.

5. Mr. Lester has $8,349 to invest in artwork. He buys a painting for $5,245 and a statue for $1,750. How much more can he invest?
   A) $1,354
   B $1,445
   C $2,300
   D $3,005

6. Which is the answer if you round the numbers to the nearest thousand and then subtract them?
   F 5,000   6,709
   G 4,000   −4,206
   H) 3,000
   J 2,000

7. The health club bought new equipment. They bought treadmills for $2,975 and exercise bikes for $2,835. How much did they spend?
   A $5,410   C $5,800
   B $5,645   D) $5,810

8. What number comes after nine million, ninety-nine thousand, ninety-nine?
   F ten million
   G) nine million, ninety-nine thousand, one hundred
   H nine million, ninety-nine thousand
   J nine million, one hundred

9. **Write About It** Explain how you solved Problem 6.

   Possible answer: I subtracted the rounded numbers;
   _____
   7,000 − 4,000 = 3,000.

© Harcourt

Name _____

Subtract Across Zeros

Understand → Plan → Solve → Check

Write the correct answer.

1. Mr. Banker has $8,000 to invest. He puts $2,679 in the bank and buys a bond for $1,500. How much does he have to invest in stocks?

$3,821

2. Bill's car has a 36,000 mile warranty. He has already traveled 17,689 miles. How much further can he drive while the car is under warranty?

18,311 miles

3. The Weddell seal can dive 1,969 feet. The sperm whale can dive 3,773 feet. Which dives deeper, and by how many more feet?

sperm whale; 1,804 feet

4. Charlie buys two books that cost $6.99 and $4.99. How much change will Charlie get from a $20.00 bill?

$8.02

Choose the letter of the correct answer.

5. $577,052 - 524,917 = \blacksquare$

A 51,135   C 53,135
B 52,135   D 53,945

6. Which subtraction problem has a difference of 3,111?

F $8,900 - 5,799$ H $5,000 - 2,890$
G $8,900 - 5,789$ J $3,111 - 3,111$

7. In the number 6,431,598, what is the value of the digit 3?

A 300   C 30,000
B 3,000   D 300,000

8. In 1996, Central City got a total of 28 inches of snow. In 1997, it got a total of 30 inches of snow. The 1998 total was between the 1996 total and the 1997 total. About how much snow did Central City get during the three years?

F About 29 in.   H About 60 in.
G About 58 in.   J About 87 in.

9. **Write About It** Explain how you solved Problem 8.

Possible answer: The 1998 total was between 28 and 30, so I estimated the 3-year total by adding 28, 29, and 30.

Choose a Method

Write the correct answer.

1. The museum has an art budget of $1,500,000 this year. It bought two statues for $500,000 and three paintings for $600,000. How much more can the museum spend this year?

   _____ $400,000 _____

2. Bryce Canyon National Park has 35,835 acres and Mesa Verde National Park has 52,121 acres. How much land do the parks have altogether?

   _____ 87,956 acres _____

3. Alaska, the largest state, has 615,230 square miles. Is the total area of South Dakota with 77,121 square miles and Texas with 267,277 square miles bigger or smaller than Alaska?

   _____ smaller _____

4. In Vermont, Montpelier has a population of 7,856; Burlington has a population of 39,004; and Rutland has a population of 17,605. How much greater is the population of Burlington than Rutland and Montpelier together?

   _____ 13,543 _____

Choose the letter of the correct answer.

5. John thinks his car engine will last 125,000 miles. His odometer reads 63,286. How many more miles does he predict that he will be able to drive his car?

   A 71,714 miles   C 61,714 miles

   B 61,724 miles   D 61,704 miles

6. Mr. T. gets in line at the bank. There are three people ahead of him. Mr. W. has Ms. U. in front of him and Mr. V. behind him. Which is the correct order of the bank line?

   F Mr. T., Mr. W., Ms. U., Mr. V.

   G Mr. W., Ms. U., Mr. V., Mr. T.

   H Ms. U., Mr. V., Mr. W., Mr. T.

   J Ms. U., Mr. W., Mr. V., Mr. T.

7. **Write About It** What strategy did you use to solve Problem 6?

   Possible Answer: I drew a picture with 4 spaces in it for the people.

   Then I wrote in letters as I read each clue.

© Harcourt

Make Predictions

Understand ➡ Plan ➡ Solve ➡ Check

By examining information in a problem, you can often use it to make a prediction. A **prediction** is your best guess based on the information given. Read the following problem.

VOCABULARY

prediction

A newspaper office will move to a larger building in 2004 if the newspaper's circulation increases by 4,000 or more from the prior year. If the change in circulation is less than 4,000, the office will remain where it is. What do you predict will happen? Explain.

Year	Number of Copies in Circulation	Increase from Previous Year
1999	14,798	—
2000	15,430	632
2001	16,630	1,200
2002	18,935	2,305
2003	22,275	3,340

1. Examine the information in the table. Write what happened to the number of copies in circulation between the given years.

from 1999 to 2000?	It increased by 632.
from 2000 to 2001?	It increased by over 1,000.
from 2001 to 2002?	It increased by over 2,000.
from 2002 to 2003?	It increased by over 3,000.

2. Solve the problem. The office will probably move to a larger building,

since the number of copies has increased each year.

3. Describe the strategy you used. I made a prediction based on the data

given in the table.

Make a prediction based on the information given. Solve.

4. Zephyr Book Company plans to change their book covers if book sales in 2004 are less than in 2000. Do you predict they will change their book covers in 2004? Explain.

Year	Sales
1999	682,371
2000	640,023
2001	521,052
2002	402,056
2003	298,120

They will probably change the

covers, since sales have been decreasing.

© Harcourt

Expressions

Write the correct answer.

1. Six baseball players sat on the bench. One got up to bat and some more sat down. Write an expression that matches the words.

   Possible answer: $(6 - 1) + c$

2. Mario received 4 large birthday gifts and 3 small gifts. He opened two gifts. Write an expression that matches the words. How many does he have left to open?

   $(4 + 3) - 2; 5$

3. Ms. Smith's class collected 4,326 juice cans and 6,859 soda cans. How many more soda cans than juice cans did they collect?

   2,533 soda cans

4. Byron had 18 newspapers. He delivered 5 on Fair Way and 7 on Post Road. How many newspapers does he have now?

   6 newspapers

Choose the letter of the correct answer.

5. Mary made 6 chocolate chip cookies and 7 sugar cookies. Mike ate 3. Which expression matches the words?

   A $(6 + 7) + 3$
   B $(6 - 3) + 7$
   C $6 + (7 + 3)$
   D $(6 + 7) - 3$

6. The tomato plant had 6 blossoms on Sunday and on Monday a rabbit ate 2 blossoms. On Tuesday 3 more blossoms grew. Which expression matches the words?

   F $6 - (3 - 2)$
   G $6 - (2 - 3)$
   H $(6 - 2) + 3$
   J $(6 - 3) + 2$

7. Round 48,597 to the greatest place value.

   A 48,000
   B 48,600
   C 49,000
   D 50,000

8. The population of Greenville was 48,299. Now it is 54,812. How much has it grown?

   F 6,513 people
   G 6,843 people
   H 6,947 people
   J 7,943 people

Name _____

Addition Properties

Write the correct answer.

Understand ➡ Plan ➡ Solve ➡ Check

1. Change the order or group the addends to add (18 + 11) + 29 mentally. Find the sum.

   _____18 + (11 + 19); 48_____

2. Riley has saved $65.00. He buys a book for $4.50 and a game for $29.99. How much money does he have left?

   _____$30.51_____

3. Write the number 106,510 in word form.

   one hundred six thousand, five

   _____hundred ten_____

4. Find the missing number. Name the Addition Property you used.

   135 + __?__ = 135

   _____0; Identity_____

Choose the letter of the correct answer.

5. Which property of addition does the number sentence show?

   13 + 4 = 4 + 13

   A Associative Property
   B Commutative Property
   C Distributive Property
   D Identity Property

6. What is the standard form for the number forty-five million, two hundred fifty thousand, three hundred twelve?

   F 4,525,312
   G 4,205,312
   H 45,250,312
   J 45,205,312

7. Which shows the numbers in order from *greatest* to *least*?

   A 31,105; 31,152; 31,085
   B 31,152; 31,105; 31,085
   C 31,085; 31,152; 31,105
   D 31,152; 31,085; 31,105

8. Which number sentence shows an example of the Associative Property of Addition?

   F 0 + 55 = 55
   G 32 + 24 + 14 = 32 + 14 + 24
   H 12 + 16 = 16 + 12
   J (24 + 6) + 5 = 24 + (6 + 5)

9. **Write About It** Explain the Addition Property you used in Problem 1.

   Possible answer: I used the Associative Property of Addition. This
   property states that the way addends are grouped does not change
   the sum.

Equations

Write the correct answer.

Understand → Plan → Solve → Check

1. Use mental math to solve the equation. Check your solution.

$n + 9 = 16$

_____ $n = 7$ _____

2. Find the value of the expression if $c = 4$ and $d = 7$.

$(c + 6) - (d + 1)$

_____ 2 _____

3. Juan had 22 clay animals and got more for his birthday. He now has 25. Write an equation and choose a variable for the unknown.

_____ $22 + a = 25$ _____

4. What is the missing number in the pattern?

7, 10, 13, 16, __, 22

_____ 19 _____

Choose the letter of the correct answer.

5. The 25 students in Mrs. Dona's class took a trip. The 14 girls boarded the bus first. How many boys were left to board the bus?

A 9   **C** 14
B 11   **D** 25

6. What is the most reasonable estimate of the sum?

$478 + 778 + 994 = $ __?__

F 2,000   **H** 2,300
G 2,100   **J** 2,500

7. William had some marbles. He gave 3 marbles away and has seven left. Which equation describes the situation?

A $m + 3 = 7$
B $7 + 3 = m$
C $7 - m = 3$
D $m - 3 = 7$

8. I am thinking of a number with 7 tens more than 4,339. Which equation best describes this number?

F $n + 7 = 4,339$
G $n + 70 = 4,339$
H $4,339 + 7 = n$
J $4,339 + 70 = n$

9. Write About It Explain how you solved Problem 4.

I found that the difference between the pairs of numbers

was 3, so I added 3 to 16.

Patterns: Find a Rule

Understand ➡ Plan ➡ Solve ➡ Check

Write the correct answer.

1. Find the rule. Write the rule as an equation.

x		y
5	→	10
10	→	15
15	→	20

add 5; $x + 5 = y$

2. Find the rule. Write the rule as an equation.

x		y
14	→	10
19	→	15
24	→	20

subtract 4; $x - 4 = y$

3. Sarah has a stamp collection with 254 stamps. She gave some to her brother. Write an expression to describe the number of stamps she has left.

$254 - s$

4. Sam has 10 friends coming to his house. He takes 5 glasses from one cabinet and 2 from another. Write an expression to show how many more he will need.

$10 - (5 + 2)$

Choose the letter of the correct answer.

5. If the rule is $w + 15 = z$ and $w = 24$, what is the value of z?

   A 9

   B 29

   C 31

   (D) 39

6. What is the rule?

   2, 4, 6, 8, 10, 12, . . .

   (F) add 2

   G add 4

   H subtract 3

   J subtract 4

7. Which is true?

   A 1,942 < 1429

   B 4,912 > 4,921

   (C) 9,142 > 9,124

   D 9,421 < 9,412

8. What number is next?

   19, 28, 37, 46 _____

   F 45   (H) 55

   G 54   J 57

9. **Write About It** What strategy did you use to solve Problem 6?

   Possible answer: I looked at the pattern and saw that each number

   increased by 2.

Balance Equations

Write the correct answer.

1. Tell whether the values are equal. Find the value on each side.

   3 nickels + 1 dime = 1 quarter

   yes; $0.25 = $0.25

2. Ed had 3 quarters and 1 dime. He gave $0.50 to his friend. How much does he have left?

   35 cents

3. Mary has 1 dime and 3 quarters. Joe has 4 dimes and 6 nickels. Do they have the same amount of money? Explain.

   No, Mary has 85 cents, and Joe has 70 cents.

4. Glenn has 6 more books than Bob. Bob has 4 fewer than Sue. If Sue has 10 books, how many books does Glenn have?

   12 books

Choose the letter of the correct answer.

5. Which equation would be true if ▇ = 4?

   A 5 + ▇ = 4 + 6

   B 6 − ▇ = 12 − 4

   C ▇ + 4 = 2 + 6

   D 5 + 4 = ▇ + 3

6. In an election, Jones had 12,345 votes, Edwards had 12,453 votes and Smith had 12,436 votes. Who had the greatest number of votes?

   F Edwards

   G Jones

   H Smith

   J Williams

7. Which does not equal 80¢?

   A 3 quarters, 1 nickel

   B 2 quarters, 3 dimes

   C 5 dimes, 20 pennies

   D 14 nickels, 10 pennies

8. Our product is 96. Our sum is 20. Who are we?

   F 6 and 14

   G 6 and 16

   H 8 and 12

   J 9 and 11

9. **Write About It** How did you solve Problem 5?

   Possible answer: I substituted 4 for ▇ in each

   expression. A, 9 < 10; B, 2 < 8; C, 8 = 8; D, 9 > 7

Form Mental Images

Understand → Plan → Solve → Check

Drawing a picture can help you **visualize**, or form mental images of what a problem is describing. As you read the problem, draw a picture of what is being described. Read the following problem.

VOCABULARY

visualize

> At the flower shop, the plants are in 3 rows of 2 boxes in each row. There are 4 plants in each box. How many plants are there in all?

1. Draw a picture to show what is being described in each part of the problem.

Problem	Visualize/Use a Picture
At the flower shop, the plants are in 3 rows of 2 boxes in each row.	Check students' drawings.
There are 4 plants in each box.	

2. Solve the problem. $(3 \times 2) \times 4 = 24$; 24 plants

3. Describe the strategy you used. Possible answer: I multiplied 3×2, and then multiplied 6×4 to get 24.

Draw a picture to visualize and solve each problem. Check students' drawings.

4. The rose bouquets at the flower shop are in 3 rows of 3. Janice put 3 more bouquets in each row. In all, how many bouquets of roses are there?

   18 bouquets

5. Bob made 2 identical flower arrangements. Each one had 4 carnations and 4 roses. How many flowers did Bob use?

   16 flowers

© Harcourt

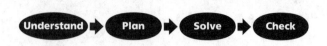

Telling Time

Write the correct answer.

Understand ➜ Plan ➜ Solve ➜ Check

1. Write *seconds*, *minutes*, *hours*, or *days* to describe the unit you would use to measure the amount of time it takes to read this math problem.

_____ seconds _____

2. Write the time shown on the clock. Include seconds.

_____ 7:14 and 27 seconds _____

3. In the 1970s, Chesterfield had 13,998 mm of snowfall. In the 1980s it had 5,390 mm and in the 1990s it had 11,302 mm. Write the years in order from the greatest snowfall to the least.

_____ 1970s, 1990s, 1980s _____

4. The town budget of Chesterfield is thirteen million, three hundred ninety-five thousand, eight hundred eleven dollars. Write this amount in standard form.

_____ $13,395,811 _____

Choose the letter of the correct answer.

5. It is 26 minutes until noon lunch. What time is shown on the digital clock?

   A 1:30   C 11:34
   B 5:44   D 12:26

6. A digital clock shows 3:42. Which letter shows the same time?

   F 42 minutes before 3
   G 42 minutes past 3
   H 18 minutes before 2
   J 34 minutes before 2

7. What is the value of 5 dimes, 5 quarters and 5 nickels?

   A 15¢   C $1.75
   B 55¢   D $2.00

8. How much greater is 46,010 than 45,999?

   F 1,001   H 21
   G 121   J 11

9. **Write About It** Explain why you chose the answer you did for Problem 5.

Possible answer: I used a clock face and counted back 26 minutes from 12:00.

© Harcourt

Name _____

Elapsed Time

Understand ➡ Plan ➡ Solve ➡ Check

Write the correct answer.

1. Vijay and Claudia were born on the same day in the same city in the same year. Vijay was born at 8:56 A.M. Claudia was born 6 hours and 25 minutes later than Vijay. What time was Claudia born?

3:21 P.M.

2. Henry has a rock collection. He buys 7 more rocks at a rock shop. Let r represent the number of rocks in Henry's collection before he visited the rock shop. Write an expression for the number of rocks he has in his collection now.

$r + 7$

3. Last year, students collected 1,256 aluminum cans to recycle. This year they collected 2,579 cans. How many more cans did they collect this year?

1,323 cans

4. Renee watches a movie that starts at 5:45 P.M. The movie ends at 7:35 P.M. How long is the movie?

1 hr 50 min

Choose the letter of the correct answer.

5. The clock in Nancy's car shows 10:07 when she leaves home in the morning. That afternoon when she arrives home, it shows 2:39. How much time has elapsed?

  A 2 hr 46 min   C 4 hr 32 min
  B 3 hr 32 min   D 4 hr 46 min

6. Karl counts 128 CDs on a shelf in the school media center. If there is another shelf holding 194 CDs, what is a reasonable estimate of the total number of CDs?

  F 600   H 300
  G 550   J 150

7. Which shows the numbers in order from least to greatest?

  A 1,340   1,430   1,403
  B 1,340   1,403   1,430
  C 1,430   1,403   1,340
  D 1,403   1,340   1,430

8. Roger worked on his homework for 1 hour and 49 minutes. If he started at 3:33 P.M., at what time did he finish?

  F 4:16 P.M.   H 5:16 P.M.
  G 4:22 P.M.   J 5:22 P.M.

9. **Write About It** Explain why you chose the answer you did for Problem 5.

Possible answer: I skip-counted to get from 10:07 to 2:07 and from 2:07 to 2:39. This gave me 4 hours and 32 minutes.

© Harcourt

Name _____

Sequence Information

Understand ➔ Plan ➔ Solve ➔ Check

Putting events in order, or **sequencing the information,** can help you solve a problem. You can use sequence clues to determine the order of events in a problem. Look for words such as *first, second, last, next, then, now, before, after,* and *already.* Read the following problem.

VOCABULARY

sequence information

Deana wants to go swimming for 2 hours Saturday afternoon, but before that she has to get her hair cut. She needs to be home for dinner by 6:30 P.M. If Deana's haircut is scheduled for 1:30 and takes 45 minutes, will she have time to visit Kathy for 2 hours and then take 20 minutes to drive home?

1. List each activity and its length in order.

Event 1: _Hair cut: 45 min_____   Event 2: Swimming: 2 hours

Event 3: _Visit Kathy: 2 hours_____   Event 4: _Drive home: 20 min_____

2. List the starting and ending times of each event.

Event	Start Time	End Time
Hair Cut	1:30 P.M.	2:15 P.M.
Swimming	2:15 P.M.	4:15 P.M.
Visit Kathy	4:15 P.M.	6:15 P.M.
Drive Home	6:15 P.M.	6:35 P.M.

The schedule shows that Deana will not be able to do all the things she wants to do and still be home for dinner at 6:30 P.M.

Use sequencing to help solve these problems.

3. Mr. Zapata is working from 12:00 P.M. until 6:00 P.M. He has a two-hour meeting at 3:30 P.M. He needs to make two 30-minute phone calls and write two memos that will take one hour each. Can he do everything? Explain.

Yes; check students' explanations.

4. Zoe is taking a cross-country trip. She is going to leave on May 1. She has to be in Santa Fe on May 8. It will take her 3 days to drive to Dallas, where she wants to visit a friend for 5 days, then make the 2-day trip to Santa Fe. Can she do it? Explain.

No; check students' explanations.

Elapsed Time on a Calendar

Understand ➡ Plan ➡ Solve ➡ Check

Write the correct answer.

March						
S	M	T	W	T	F	S
		1	2	3	4	5
6	7	8	9	10	11	12
13	14	15	16	17	18	19
20	21	22	23	24	25	26
27	28	29	30	31		

April						
S	M	T	W	T	F	S
					1	2
3	4	5	6	7	8	9
10	11	12	13	14	15	16
17	18	19	20	21	22	23
24	25	26	27	28	29	30

May						
S	M	T	W	T	F	S
1	2	3	4	5	6	7
8	9	10	11	12	13	14
15	16	17	18	19	20	21
22	23	24	25	26	27	28
29	30	31				

1. Use the calendars above. Write the day of the week that is 5 days after March 4.

   _____Wednesday_____

2. Use the calendars above. Write the date that is exactly 6 weeks before May 18.

   _____April 6_____

3. Nyla starts her workout at 10:45 A.M. She works out for 1 hour and 18 minutes. What time is it when she ends her workout?

   _____12:03 P.M._____

4. Chuck scored 88, 97, 87, 88, 99, 90, and 97 on his first 7 math tests. What is the median of these scores?

   _____90_____

Choose the letter of the correct answer.

5. Which digit is in the ten millions place of 583,129,450?

   A 8   C 4

   B 5   D 2

6. Use the calendars at the top of the page. Which date is 24 days after March 20?

   F April 10   H April 12

   G April 11   J April 13

7. Ella looks at her digital clock. She sees that the number of minutes is 2 times the number of hours. The sum of the digits is 15. What time is it?

   A 4:08   C 7:08

   B 6:12   D 8:16

8. Use the calendars at the top of the page. How many days after the first day of April is the last Monday in May?

   F 62 days   H 60 days

   G 61 days   J 59 days

9. **Write About It** Explain how you solved Problem 7.

   Possible answer: I made an organized list: 1:02, 2:04, 3:06, 4:08, 5:10, 6:12, 7:14, 8:16, 9:18, 10:20, and 11:22. Then I found the sum of the digits of each.

Collect and Organize Data

Understand → Plan → Solve → Check

Write the correct answer.

1. Use the frequency table. How many stars did Chas identify on Thursday night?

STARS I IDENTIFIED EACH NIGHT

Night	Frequency (Number of Stars)	Cumulative Frequency
Wed	22	22
Thurs	28	50
Fri	46	96

28 stars

2. Use the frequency table from Problem 1. By the end of Thursday night, how many stars had Chas identified in all?

50 stars

3. On which night did Chas identify the greatest number of stars?

Friday night

Choose the letter of the correct answer.

4. Use the frequency table below. On which day did the fewest number of students sign up?

BASKETBALL PRACTICE SIGN-UP

Day	Frequency (Number of Students)	Cumulative Frequency
Mon	12	12
Tues	15	27
Wed	9	36
Thurs	41	77

A Monday   C Tuesday
B Wednesday   D Thursday

5. Use the frequency table from Problem 4. How many students signed up during the first three days?

F 12   G 15   H 36   J 42

6. Joan's car goes 420 miles on a tank of gas. She needs to make a 1,480-mile trip. What is the least number of tanks of gas she will need?

A 1   B 2   C 3   D 4

7. **Write About It** Explain the difference between the frequency column and the cumulative frequency column in a frequency table.

Possible answer: The frequency column tells the number that occurs in each

period; the cumulative column shows the total number that have occurred.

© Harcourt

Find Mean, Median, and Mode

Understand ➡ Plan ➡ Solve ➡ Check

For 1–4, use the Pennies Collected for Charity table.
Write the correct answer.

1. What is the median?
   What is the mode?

   _____ $4.00: $4.00 _____

2. What is the mean?

   _____ $5.00 _____

PENNIES COLLECTED FOR CHARITY	
DAY	**AMOUNT**
Monday	$4.00
Tuesday	$2.00
Wednesday	$8.00
Thursday	$7.00
Friday	$4.00

3. What was the total amount of
   money collected?

   _____ $25.00 _____

4. Suppose $6 was collected on
   Saturday. Would the mode or the
   median change? Explain?
   The mode would still be $4.00
   but the median would be $5.00.

Choose the letter of the correct answer.

For 5–6, use the table.
The table shows the number of goals
the Flash soccer team scored.

GOALS FLASH SOCCER TEAM SCORED				
Game	1	2	3	4
Goals	3	9	3	5

5. What is the median number
   of goals?

   A 3   **C** 5
   B 4   **D** 9

6. What is the mean number of
   goals?

   F 3   **H** 5
   G 4   **J** 9

7. Round 183,473 to the nearest
   thousand.

   A 180,000   **C** 184,000
   B 183,000   **D** 190,000

8. Use the Pennies Collected for
   Charity table. How much less
   money was collected on Thursday
   than Wednesday?

   F $1.00   **H** $3.00
   G $2.00   **J** $4.00

9. **Write About It** How did you find your answer to Problem 6?

   Possible answer: I found the sum of the number of goals. Then I divided
   by 4.

Name _____

Read Line Plots

Write the correct answer.

Understand ➡ Plan ➡ Solve ➡ Check

1. Each X on the line plot stands for one student. How many students watched 4 movies?

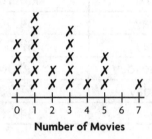

Number of Movies

1 student
_____

2. Chris swam 30 laps at swim team practice. Then he swam some more. Write an expression to show how many total laps Chris swam.

$30 + x$
_____

3. Order 88,416; 88,614; 86,418 and 88,641 from *greatest* to *least*.

88,641; 88,614; 88,416; 86,418
_____

4. What is the range of the data in the line plot in Problem 1?

7
_____

Choose the letter of the correct answer.

5. In the line plot from Problem 1, which number of movies did the greatest number of students see?

A 0   Ⓑ 1   C 2   D 3

6. In the line plot from Problem 1, how many students watched 2 movies?

F 0   G 1   Ⓗ 2   J 3

7. Kerri spent a total of $25.00 at the pet store. She spent $8.00 on chew toys for her dogs, and the rest on two bags of dog food. The price was the same for both bags. How much did she spend for one bag of dog food?

A $7.00   C $10.00
Ⓑ $8.50   D $17.00

8. Write About It Describe the steps you took to solve Problem 7.

Possible answer: I subtracted
_____

$8.00 from $25.00 to find the
_____

amount spent on both bags,
_____

then divided by 2 for the amount
_____

spent on one bag.
_____

© Harcourt

PS28   Problem Solving

Make Stem-and-Leaf Plots

Understand ➡ Plan ➡ Solve ➡ Check

Write the correct answer.

1. The stem-and-leaf plot shows the science test scores of Ms. Sitomer's students. What is the median of the scores?

**SCIENCE TEST:
MS. SITOMER'S CLASS**

Stem	Leaves
7	0 2 2 4 8 9
8	0 0 3 3 4 5 9 9 9
9	0 1 1 2 3 5 8 9

85

2. Central City voters were asked what they thought was the city's most important issue. Which issue got the most votes?

WHAT IS CENTRAL CITY'S MOST IMPORTANT ISSUE?

Issue	Votes
Crime	32
Land Use	14
Poverty	35
Taxes	29

Poverty

3. Use the stem-and-leaf plot. What were the highest and lowest scores on the test?

99 and 70

4. Use the survey. Each person surveyed chose one issue. How many people were surveyed?

110 people

Choose the letter of the correct answer.

5. Use the stem-and-leaf plot. What is the total number of students in Ms. Sitomer's class who took the science test?

A 23   **B** 24   **C** 26   **D** 30

6. Use the stem-and-leaf plot. What is the mode of the scores?

F 9   **G** 80   **H** 85   **J** 89

7. Ollie makes a pay-phone call that costs $0.75 for the first 3 minutes and $0.15 for each additional minute. Ollie's call costs him $2.10. How long did he talk?

A 12 min   **C** 9 min
B 10 min   **D** 8 min

8. Write About It Explain how you found your answer to Problem 7.

Possible answer: I made a prediction and then tested it. My total was greater than (or less than) $2.10, so I selected a lesser (or greater) number.

© Harcourt

Name _____

Compare Graphs

Understand ➡ Plan ➡ Solve ➡ Check

Write the correct answer.

1. How could you make the graph below easier to read?

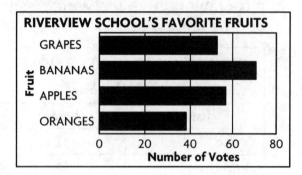

RIVERVIEW SCHOOL'S FAVORITE FRUITS

GRAPES
BANANAS
APPLES
ORANGES

Fruit

0   20   40   60   80
Number of Votes

Possible answer:

Change the interval to 5.

3. How would the graph in Problem 1 change if the interval were 10?

It would be much easier to read

the differences between the

3 longest bars.

2. Suppose the bars in the graph in Problem 1 were drawn vertically. What would the tallest bar represent?

the most popular fruit (bananas)

4. Cinzia spent 3 days of her vacation at the beach and 4 days at her grandparents' house. She spent the rest of her 10-day vacation at home. Write an equation to model this.

$3 + 4 + x = 10$

Choose the letter of the correct answer.

5. Gary builds an upside-down pyramid with blocks. He puts 1 block in the first layer, 4 blocks in the second, and 9 blocks in the third. How many blocks would go in the sixth layer?

   A 24   B 30   C 36   D 45

6. In the graph in Problem 1, which fruit received about 40 votes?

   F bananas   H apples
   G grapes   J oranges

7. Which is the best estimate of the total number of votes cast for all four fruits in the graph in Problem l?

   A 210   B 320   C 380   D 420

8. **Write About It** Describe the rule for the pattern in Problem 5.

   The number of blocks in a layer is equal to the number of the layer

   multiplied by itself.

Summarize

Understand ➡ Plan ➡ Solve ➡ Check

To **summarize** is to state something in a brief way. Knowing how to summarize information is a useful skill. Sometimes using a graph or a plot to display information is a good way to summarize. Read the following problem.

VOCABULARY

summarize

Sue presented this data to her classmates.

NUMBER OF DOGS IN SHOW

Size of Dog	Number of dogs
Toy	10
Small	15
Medium	25
Large	20

The class wanted to compare the different types of dogs in the show. What is the difference between the dog type with the greatest number of dogs and the dog type with the least number of dogs at the show? Explain.

---

1. Complete the graph to summarize the data in the table.

NUMBER OF DOGS IN SHOW

Size of Dog	Number of dogs
Toy	▪ ▪
Small	▪ ▪ ▪
Medium	▪ ▪ ▪ ▪ ▪
Large	▪ ▪ ▪ ▪

Key: each ___▪___ = 5 dogs

2. Solve the problem. There are the most symbols for the medium size dogs, 25 dogs, and the least for toy dogs, 10 dogs: 25 − 10 = 15. There were 15 more medium size dogs than toy dogs at the show.

3. Describe the strategy you used. Possible answer: I summarized the information in the pictograph.

© Harcourt

Make Bar and Double-Bar Graphs

Write the correct answer.

Eye Color	Fourth Graders	Fifth Graders
Brown	12	9
Blue	6	13
Green or Hazel	10	7

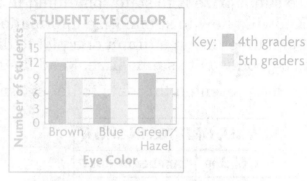

STUDENT EYE COLOR

Key: ■ 4th graders
■ 5th graders

Number of Students

15 12 9 6 3 0

Brown Blue Green/ Hazel

Eye Color

1. Use the data to write the best scale and interval for a double-bar graph.

Answers may vary.

2. Make a double-bar graph for the data.

3. Round 987,654 to the nearest ten thousand.

990,000

4. Write an equation. There were 9 cats in the shelter. Some were adopted. Now there are 4 cats.

$9 - n = 4$

Choose the letter of the correct answer.

5. Use your bar graph. Which eye color did more 5th graders have than 4th graders?

A Brown   C Green/Hazel
B Blue   D Red

6. Estimate.   48,670
                  −12,600

F 60,000   H 40,000
G 50,000   J 30,000

7. Use your bar graph. Which eye color did the fewest 5th graders have?

A Brown   C Green/Hazel
B Blue   D Red

8. Evaluate: $(20 - 3) - (4 - 1)$

F 20   H 13
G 14   J 12

9. **Write About It** Explain how you chose a scale and interval in Problem 1.

Possible answer: The data ranges from 6 to 13, so I chose a scale of

0 to 15; an interval of 3 makes 6, 9, and 12 fall on the lines.

© Harcourt

Read Line Graphs

Write the correct answer.

1. Use the graph. What is Horseville's average July temperature?

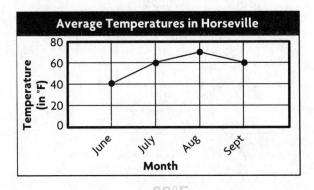

Average Temperatures in Horseville

60°F
_____

2. Use the survey table. During which two weeks were there the same number of absences?

FEBRUARY ABSENCES AT DIERKER SCHOOL	
Week	**Absences**
1	13
2	15
3	21
4	15

Weeks 2 and 4
_____

3. Use the graph. During which month is the average Horseville temperature about 70°F?

August
_____

4. Use the survey table. What was the total number of absences during February?

64 absences
_____

Choose the letter of the correct answer.
For 5–6, use the graph.

5. Which month had an average temperature of 40°F?

A June **C** August
B July **D** September

For 7–8, use the table.

7. How many more absences were there in Week 3 than in Week 1?

A 21 **B** 12 **C** 8 **D** 6

6. Which month had the highest average temperature?

F June **H** August
G July **J** September

8. During which week were there the most absences?

F Week 1 **H** Week 3
G Week 2 **J** Week 4

9. Write About It Explain how you got your answer to Problem 6.

Possible answer: I looked for the highest point on the line graph.
_____

_____

Make Line Graphs

Write the correct answer.

Understand ➡ Plan ➡ Solve ➡ Check

1. Make a line graph to show this data.

HERITAGE MUSEUM	
Month	**Visitors**
May	900
June	1,500
July	1,300
August	1,100
September	1,000

Check students' graphs.

2. Write a rule and an equation for the input/output table.

Input	Output
y	*z*
4	16
2	8
5	20
3	12

multiply by 4; $y \times 4 = z$

Write the correct answer.

3. What was the total attendance at the museum in the summer months of June, July, and August?

3,900 visitors

4. Order from *greatest* to *least*: 45,892; 4,392; 483,394; 393,303

483,394; 393,303; 45,892; 4,392

Choose the letter of the correct answer.

5. In what month did the fewest people visit the museum?

A May C July
B September D August

6. What is the value of the digit 7 in 370,304,204?

F 70 million H 70 thousand
G 7 million J 70

7. Which trend does your graph show?

A Museum attendance was greatest in the summer months.
B The number of visitors decreased from May to June.
C The number of visitors increased from June to July.
D Most visitors came in January.

8. What is the word form of 300,012?

F three hundred twelve thousand
G three hundred thousand and twelve
H three hundred thousand, twelve
J three hundred, twelve

9. **Write About It** Explain how you got your answer to Problem 7.

Possible answer: I looked at the graph to see which one is true.

Make Circle Graphs

Understand ➡ Plan ➡ Solve ➡ Check

Write the correct answer.

FAVORITE EXERCISE	
Exercise	Number of Votes
Pushups	40
Pull Ups	10
Sit Ups	30

FAVORITE EXERCISE

1. How many sections would be best to use for a circle graph for the data?

    <u>8 sections</u>

2. Make a circle graph for the data.

    Check students' graphs.

3. Write one hundred four thousand, twenty in number form.

    104,020

4. Write 86,539 in expanded form.

    80,000 + 6,000+ 500+ 30+ 9

Choose the letter of the correct answer.

For 5–6, use the table above.

5. How many people voted for a favorite exercise?

    A 20 people   C 50 people
    B 30 people   D 80 people

6. How many more people chose sit ups than pull ups as their favorite exercise?

    F 10 people   H 30 people
    G 20 people   J 50 people

7. Which number is *greater* than 5,372,000?

    A 5,299,999   C 5,359,560
    B 5,400,000   D 5,099,896

8. What is the value of $36 - (5 + 4)$?

    F 37   H 28
    G 36   J 27

9. **Write About It** Explain how you got your answer to Problem 5.

    Possible answer: I added the number of votes for Pushups, Pull Ups,

    and Sit Ups.

Choose an Appropriate Graph

Understand ➡ Plan ➡ Solve ➡ Check

Write the correct answer.

1. Write whether you would use a *line graph*, *bar graph*, or *stem-and-leaf plot* to show how the price of a gallon of milk changes each month over a year.

line graph

2. Write whether you would use a *line graph*, *bar graph*, or *stem-and-leaf plot* to show the types of pets your classmates have.

bar graph

3. The stem-and-leaf plot shows the longest bike trip each student of the fourth-grade class has taken. What is the median distance?

12 miles

4. Use the stem-and-leaf plot. Write the mode of the distances.

10 miles

LONGEST BIKE TRIPS OF THE FOURTH-GRADE CLASS (in miles)

Stem	Leaves
0	0 0 3 5 8
1	0 0 0 0 0 2 2 5 5 5
2	0 0 5 5 5 5
3	0
4	5

Choose the letter of the correct answer.

5. Which type of display would be the best to show the changes in daily class attendance for the month?

   A bar graph
   B line graph
   C stem-and-leaf plot
   D NOT HERE

6. Tommy recorded his high jumps: 48 in., 55 in., 40 in., 58 in., and 55 in. He wants to show this on a bar graph. What would be the best interval for his graph?

   F 1 in.   H 50 in.
   G 5 in.   J 100 in.

7. Use the stem-and-leaf plot. How many fourth graders rode 25 miles?

   A 3   B 4   C 7   D 9

8. Which type of graph would best organize the list of ages of people at a family reunion?

   F bar graph   H stem-and-leaf plot
   G line graph J line plot

9. **Write About It** Explain your choice in Problem 8.

   Possible answer: A stem-and-leaf plot is good for organizing lists of

   numbers by place value.

© Harcourt

Draw Conclusions

Understand ➡ Plan ➡ Solve ➡ Check

A table can display a large amount of data. Looking at a graph of the data makes it easier to draw conclusions about the data.

VOCABULARY
drawing
conclusions

When you examine the graph and use what you already know to solve a problem, you are **drawing conclusions**. Read the following problem.

Jamie looked at the graph to compare the numbers of each type of animal available at two pet stores. She knows that stores that specialize in birds are more likely to carry her favorite brand of bird food.

In which store should Jamie look for the bird food?

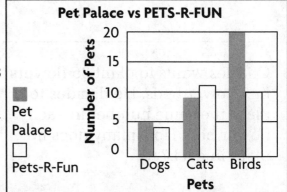

Pet Palace vs PETS-R-FUN

What Jamie Sees on the Graph	What She Concludes
Pet Palace has about the same numbers of dogs and cats as Pets-R-Fun.	The stores are about the same size.
Pet Palace has many more birds than Pets-R-Fun.	Stores with many more birds than other stores of the same size specialize in birds.

Since Jamie has concluded that Pet Palace specializes in birds, she should look for the food there.

Use the graph. Draw conclusions to solve.

Possible answers are given.

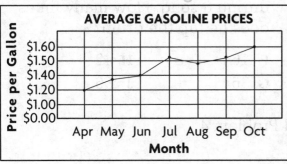

AVERAGE GASOLINE PRICES

1. Which month was best for the Lockwood family to take their car trip across the country? Explain.

   April; prices are lowest

2. In which month was a new law probably passed raising the tax on gasoline? Explain.

   June; there is a big increase in price between June and July.

Relate Multiplication and Division

Write the correct answer.

1. Write a related multiplication fact.

   $$18 \div 3 = 6$$

   _____
   $3 \times 6 = 18$, or $6 \times 3 = 18$

2. Write the fact family for the numbers 4, 7, and 28.

   _____
   $4 \times 7 = 28, 7 \times 4 = 28,$
   _____
   $28 \div 7 = 4, 28 \div 4 = 7$

3. Charles wants to plant 35 flowers in 5 flower beds. He decides to plant the same number in each flower bed. How many does he plant in each?

   _____
   7 flowers

4. Didi made an $11.87 purchase. She gave the cashier a $20.00 bill. The cashier gave her $6.13 in change. Did the cashier give her the correct change? Explain.

   _____
   no; $20.00 − $11.87 = $8.13

Choose the letter of the correct answer.

5. Which multiplication fact could you use to help you find the quotient of $36 \div 9$?

   A $6 \times 6 = 36$ **C** $4 \times 9 = 36$
   B $2 \times 2 = 4$ **D** $3 \times 3 = 9$

6. A car is driven around a 4-mile racetrack 4 times. Which can you use to find the total number of miles the car travels?

   F $4 + 4$ **H** $16 - 4$
   G 4×4 **J** $8 \div 4$

7. Dan sells a total of 32 candy bars to 8 neighbors. Each neighbor buys the same number of candy bars. How many candy bars does each buy?

   A 2   **C** 4
   B 3   **D** 5

8. Blaise is playing a bongo drum. He taps the drum with his right hand 3 times, his left hand 1 time, then his right hand 2 times. He repeats this pattern 6 times during a song. How many times does he tap the drum?

   F 16   **H** 42
   G 36   **J** 56

9. **Write About It** Explain how you solved Problem 4.

   Possible answer: I estimated $20 − $6 = $14; this is not close enough to
   _____
   $11.87, so the amount of change is incorrect.
   _____

Multiply and Divide Facts Through 5

Write the correct answer.

1. MaryJo went to a 2:10 P.M. movie. It was over at 4:32 P.M. How long was the movie?

_____2 hr 22 min_____

2. What are the median and mode of the following data?

10,11,11,12,12,13,13,13,18

_____Median is 12. Mode is 13._____

3. Label the number line to find 5 × 3.

0　　5　　10　　15

_____Check students' work._____

4. Write a related multiplication fact.

12 ÷ 3 = 4

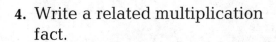

_____3 × 4 = 12_____

Choose the letter of the correct answer.

5. Carly is in a weight-lifting program and wants to graph the improvement in the amount she can lift over a period of months. What is the most appropriate graph to use?

A Stem and leaf　　**C** Bar graph
B Line graph　　　**D** Pictograph

6. Charlene counts her pennies by placing them in piles of ten. She makes 4 piles. Which shows how much money Charlene has?

F 4 + 10　　　**H** 4 × 10
G 10 − 4　　　**J** 10 ÷ 4

7. If 3 × 4 = 12, then 12 ÷ 3 = ■

A 2　　　**C** 4
B 3　　　**D** 5

8. Solve.
■ ÷ 7 = 5

F 35　　　**H** 21
G 28　　　**J** 10

9. Write About It Explain how using a number line can help you find the product in Problem 3.

_____Possible answer: I can see a pattern and can count by 5's to find the_____

_____product._____

Multiply and Divide Facts Through 10

Write the correct answer.

1. Jimmy spent 4 hours and 20 minutes driving from Cleveland to Pittsburgh. He left Cleveland at 2:50 P.M. At what time did he arrive in Pittsburgh?

   7:10 P.M.

2. Find the value of n. Write a related equation.

   $$42 \div n = 7$$

   Possible answer: _____

   $n = 6$; $7 \times 6 = 42$

3. Find the product. Show the strategy you used.
   8×7

   56; Strategies will vary.

4. A concert attracts 30,000 fans. The hall has only 22,500 seats. How many fans will *not* get in to the concert?

   7,500 fans

Choose the letter of the correct answer.

5. In the number 653,218, what digit is in the hundreds place?

   A 1
   B 2
   C 3
   D 6

6. Find the median.
   127, 143, 251, 197, 143, 154, 182

   F 143
   G 154
   H 171
   J 182

7. Travas earned the following scores on his past five math tests: 92, 83, 85, 76, 89. What is his average test grade in math?

   A 85
   B 86
   C 87
   D 88

8. Which of the following equations is *not* in the fact family for 4, 2, and 8?

   F $4 \times 2 = 8$
   G $2 \times 4 = 8$
   H $8 \div 2 = 4$
   J $4 \div 2 = 2$

9. **Write About It** What other strategy could you have used to solve Problem 3?

   Possible answer: Use break-apart to break 8×7 into 4×7 and 4×7.

   Then add $28 + 28$ to get 56.

© Harcourt

Multiplication Table Through 12

Understand ➡ Plan ➡ Solve ➡ Check

Write the correct answer.

1. Find the value of the variable. Write a related equation.

   $12 \times n = 60$

   _____5; possible answer:_____

   _____$5 \times 12 = 60$_____

2. Write 862,092 in word form.

   _____Eight hundred sixty-two_____

   _____thousand, ninety-two_____

3. Write the fact family for 7, 8, and 56.

   _____$7 \times 8 = 56, 8 \times 7 = 56,$_____

   _____$56 \div 7 = 8, 56 \div 8 = 7$_____

4. The first six multiples of 3 are 3, 6, 9, 12, 15 and 18. What are the next six multiples of 3?

   _____21, 24, 27, 30, 33, 36_____

Choose the letter of the correct answer.

5. Joe makes $12 for each lawn that he mows. He mowed 8 lawns. How much does he make altogether?

   A $20 C $96
   B $72 D $100

6. How much time has elapsed from 8:27 A.M. to 12:20 P.M.?

   F 4 hours 53 minutes
   G 4 hours 47 minutes
   H 3 hours 53 minutes
   J 3 hours 47 minutes

7. Nigel and Linda spent $6 each on movie tickets. They also shared a large popcorn for $5. How much did they spend altogether?

   A $11 C $17
   B $16 D $22

8. Which number is *not* a multiple of 11?

   F 44
   G 99
   H 111
   J 132

9. **Write About It** Explain how you solved Problem 1.

   _____Possible answer: I used the multiplication table to find the value of *n*._____

   _____Then I wrote one equation from the fact family of 12, 5, and 60._____

Name _____

Multiplication Properties

Write the correct answer.

Understand ➡ Plan ➡ Solve ➡ Check

1. Find the product of 12 × 0. Name the property of multiplication you used.

   0; Zero Property

2. Kevin has $45.95. Timothy has $3.75 more than Kevin has. How much money does Timothy have?

   $49.70

3. Anna hikes 7 miles each day for 3 days. How many miles does she hike in all?

   21 miles

4. Show two ways to group the facors of 5 × 2 × 3 by using parentheses. Then find the product.

   (5 × 2) × 3; 5 × (2 × 3); 30

Choose the letter of the correct answer.

5. Which property of multiplication does the number sentence show?
   9 × 6 = 6 × 9

   A Associative Property
   B Commutative Property
   C Zero Property
   D Identity Property

6. What is 132 ÷ 11?

   F 10
   G 11
   H 12
   J 121

7. What is the value of 12 dimes?

   A $0.12
   B $0.60
   C $1.20
   D $12.00

8. Which number sentence shows an example of the Identity Property of Multiplication?

   F 1 × 7 = 7
   G 4 × 0 = 0
   H 8 × 3 = 3 × 8
   J (3 × 2) × 4 = 3 × (2 × 4)

9. **Write About It** Explain the Associative Property of Multiplication.

   Possible answer: The Associative Property says that you can group

   factors in different ways and the product will be the same.

© Harcourt

Choose Relevant Information

Understand → Plan → Solve → Check

Sometimes a word problem contains information that may *not* help you solve the problem. You must decide which information is **relevant**, or needed to solve the problem. Read the following problem.

VOCABULARY

relevant
not relevant

> Donna's brother Chip plays on the football team. She has been the team's statistician for two years. It is her job to record and classify all the points the team scores. This season, the team has scored 11 touchdowns, worth 6 points each; 10 field goals, worth 3 points each; 8 extra-points, worth one point each; and 2 safeties, worth 2 points each. A football game consists of 4 quarters of 15 minutes each. What is the total number of points scored this season?

1. Read each fact from the problem. Write whether the fact is *relevant* or *not relevant* to solve the problem.

   a. Donna has been the team's statistician for two years. _____ not relevant

   b. The team has scored 11 touchdowns. _____ relevant

   c. The team has scored 2 safeties. _____ relevant

   d. A quarter is 15 minutes long. _____ not relevant

   e. The team has scored 8 extra-points. _____ relevant

   f. The team has scored 10 field goals. _____ relevant

2. Solve the problem. _____ $(11 \times 6) + (10 \times 3) + (8 \times 1) + (2 \times 2) = 108$; 108 points

3. Describe the strategy you used. _____ Possible answer: I found the points earned from each type of score, then added them together.

Draw a line through the information that is not relevant. Solve.

4. Lauren's best friend lives out of state. They talked on the phone for one 5-minute call, three 10-minute calls, and two 20-minute calls. There are two phones in Lauren's house. How long did the friends talk altogether?

   _____ 75 minutes

5. Benny earns $3.00 per hour baby-sitting and $10 for shovelling a driveway. It snowed 6 inches on Monday and Benny baby-sat for 4 hours. How much money did he make baby-sitting?

   _____ $12.00

Expressions

Write the correct answer.

1. Find the value of the expression.

$7 \times 8 + 4$

_____60_____

2. Find the value of the expression.

$(25 \div 5) + (6 \times 2)$

_____17_____

3. Erin needs to earn $24. She gets paid $3 per hour baby-sitting. Erin baby-sits for 5 hours on Saturday and 4 hours on Sunday. Does she earn at least $24?

Yes, she actually earns $27 dollars.

4. John buys 4 adult's fair tickets at $8 each and 3 children's tickets at $5 each. Write an expression to match the words.

$(4 \times 8) + (3 \times 5)$

Choose the letter of the correct answer.

5. What is the value of the expression?

$20 \div 4 + 1$

A 6   **C** 4

B 5   **D** 3

6. What is the value of the expression?

$87 - (7 \times 9)$

F 720   **H** 31

G 250   **J** 24

7. Thomas needs to write the standard form for two million, three hundred five thousand, six hundred seventy. What is the correct number for Thomas?

A 2,356,700   **C** 2,305,670

B 2,350,607   **D** 2,305,607

8. Play practice was supposed to begin at 1:30 P.M., but it started 18 minutes late. It ended at 3:35 P.M. How long did play practice last?

F 2 hr 47 min   **H** 2 hr 25 min

G 2 hr 37 min   **J** 1 hr 47 min

9. Write About It Describe how you found the answer to Problem 8.

Possible answer: I added to find the starting time of 1:48, and then I

subtracted to get the elapsed time of 1 hour 47 minutes.

Name _____

Order of Operations

Write the correct answer.

1. Darren has 45 apples to use in 6 gift baskets. He puts 7 apples in each basket. Follow the order of operations to find how many apples are left.

   _____ 3 apples _____

2. The Prows are driving 1,102 miles. The first day they drive 312 miles, and the second day they drive 284 miles. How many miles do they have left to drive?

   _____ 506 miles _____

3. A sculpture by a famous artist is valued at $1,306,540. Write the value in word form.

   one million, three hundred six

   thousand, five hundred forty dollars

4. Jan got 15 when she evaluated the expression 8 + 22 ÷ 2. Did she follow the order of operations? What is the correct answer?

   No, the correct answer is 19.

Choose the letter of the correct answer.

5. What is the value of 5 in 1,250,344?

   A five thousand
   B fifty thousand
   C five hundred thousand
   D fifty million

6. What is the correct order of operations to find the value of 45 − 30 ÷ 5 + 2?

   F Subtract, Divide, Add
   G Subtract, Add, Divide
   H Add, Divide, Subtract
   J Divide, Subtract, Add

7. Evaluate the expression:
   54 ÷ 6 − 3 × 2

   A 36   C 3
   B 12   D 0

8. What is the standard form of the number twenty million, five hundred sixty-four thousand, sixty-two.

   F 20,564,062   H 25,064,062
   G 20,564,620   J 200,564,620

9. **Write About It** Explain how you solved Problem 4.

   Possible answer: Jan added first instead of dividing first. The order of

   operations states that you must multiply and divide from left to right

   before you add and subtract.

Expressions and Equations with Variables

Understand ➡ Plan ➡ Solve ➡ Check

Write the correct answer.

1. Find the value of $8 \times s$ if $s = 12$.

    96

2. How much greater is 8,752,340 than 8,742,340?

    10,000

3. Order the following numbers from *greatest* to *least*: 34,871; 304,718; 34,718; 340,718; 304,817

    340,718; 304,817; 304,718;
    34,871; 34,718

4. A number of dolls divided equally among 5 shelves is 8 dolls on each shelf. Write an equation to show the total number of dolls. Tell what the variable represents.

    $d \div 5 = 8$; d is the
    total number of dolls

Choose the letter of the correct answer.

5. 72 peanuts divided into b equal groups equals 9 bags. Which expression matches the words?

    A $9 \div 72 = b$ **C** $9 - b = 72$
    B $72 \div b = 9$ **D** $9 \div b = 72$

6. It is 18 minutes before noon. What time would it show on a digital clock?

    F 11:18   **H** 12:18
    G 11:42   **J** 12:42

7. Solve the equation: $35 \div p = 5$.

    A $p = 7$ **C** $p = 30$
    B $p = 8$ **D** $p = 40$

8. Students want to collect 175 books for a shelter. Last week they collected 83 books and this week they collected 76 books. How many more books do they want to collect?

    F 334 books   **H** 92 books
    G 159 books   **J** 16 books

9. **Write About It** Explain how you solved Problem 7.

    Possible answer: I used mental math to find p.

_____

© Harcourt

Interpret Symbols

Understand ➡ Plan ➡ Solve ➡ Check

It is important to be able to interpret symbols when reading or writing a number sentence. **Interpreting symbols** means understanding what each symbol in the number sentence means. Mathematical symbols include numbers and $, ( ), +, −, ×, ÷, =, and variables such as n. Read the following problem.

VOCABULARY
interpreting symbols

> Alex bought 4 computer games. Each game cost $8.00. Then Alex bought a shirt for $18.00. Alex had $5.00 left. How much money did Alex have to start with?

Think about the problem. Tell what the bold-faced symbols stand for. Possible answers:

1. **(4 × 8)** + 18 + 5 = n 4 games at $8 each, $32 for games

   (4 × 8) **+ 18 + 5** = n plus $18 for a shirt plus $5 change

   (4 × 8) + 18 + 5 = **n** equals how much money Alex had to start

2. Solve the problem. $(4 × 8) + 18 + 5 = n$

   32 + 18 + 5 = 55; $55

3. Describe the strategy you used. Possible answer: I used symbols and worked backward.

Write a number sentence for each problem. Tell what the symbols mean. Solve.

4. Stan spent $238.50 on computer programs. Stella spent $152.75 on computer programs. How much more did Stan spend than Stella?

   $238.50 − $152.75 = n;

   amount Stan spent minus the

   amount Stella spent equals how

   much more Stan spent;

   n = $85.75

5. Jody spends 125 minutes each morning and 75 minutes each night, 3 days a month, on the Internet. How much time each month does Jody spend on the Internet?

   3 × (125 + 75) = n;

   3 days a month times the sum

   of the minutes each day equals

   the total number of minutes;

   n = 600 minutes

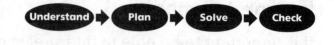
Balance Equations

Write the correct answer.

1. Lucia needs to order programs for a football game. There have been 5,883 tickets sold, but the programs can only be ordered in sets of 100. How many programs should Lucia order?

_____ 5,900 programs _____

2. Ann took 3 rolls of pictures with 12 pictures on each roll of film. When she developed them, 8 pictures were bad. Write an expression for the number of good pictures Ann took, then find its value.

_____ $(3 \times 12) - 8; 28$ _____

3. Divide both sides of the equation by 4.
$$2 \times 6 = 3 \times 4$$
What is the new value of each side?

_____ 3 _____

4. Divide both sides of the equation by 5.
$$20 \div 2 = 5 \times 2$$
What is the new value of each side?

_____ 2 _____

Choose the letter of the correct answer.

5. Joel divided both sides of this equation by a number and got a new value of 3. What number did Joel divide by?
$$18 \div 3 = 23 - 17$$

A 7　　　　　C 3
B 6　　　　　D 2

6. Elena wraps yarn around a square spindle. The spindle measures 4 inches on each side. How many inches of yarn are wrapped on the spindle when Elena has completed 4 turns around it?

F 32 inches　　H 52 inches
G 44 inches　　J 64 inches

7. When this equation is multiplied by 9, what is the new value of each side?
$$15 - 7 = 64 \div 8$$

A 45　　　　　C 63
B 54　　　　　D 72

8. Bollard has a population of 734,989 and Pollard has a population of 592,176. What is a reasonable estimate of the sum of the populations of the two towns?

F 1,500,000　　H 1,300,000
G 1,400,000　　J 1,200,000

9. **Write About It**　Explain how you arrived at your answer for Problem 6.
Possible answer: I wrote the expression $4 \times (4 + 4 + 4 + 4)$ and evaluated it to get 64.

© Harcourt

Patterns: Find a Rule

Understand ➡ Plan ➡ Solve ➡ Check

Write the correct answer.

1. Find a rule. Write the rule as an equation. Find the missing number.

Input	Output
s	b
48	■
42	7
36	6
30	5

Divide by 6; $s \div 6 = b$; 8

2. Find a rule. Write the rule as an equation. Find the missing number.

Input	Output
g	r
4	32
5	40
6	48
7	■

Multiply by 8; $g \times 8 = r$; 56

3. Put the numbers in order from *least* to *greatest*.

64,923; 64,832; 63,933; 65,834

$63,933 < 64,832 < 64,923 < 65,834$

4. A's profits were $33,494,002. B's were $50,405,986. Which earned more? How much more?

B; $16,911,984 more

Choose the letter of the correct answer.

5.

Input	z	4	5	6	7
Output	y	12	15	18	21

Which equation shows the rule?

A $z + 4 = y$ **C** $z \times 3 = y$
B $z \div y = 3$ **D** $z \times 5 = y$

6. Which equation is in the same fact family as $3 \times 8 = 24$?

F $24 \div 4 = 6$
G $2 \times 12 = 24$
H $24 \div 8 = 3$
J $24 \div 6 = 4$

7. Barbara has 103 crayons. She puts some of them into 5 boxes with 20 in each box. Which expression shows this?

A $103 - (5 \times 20)$ **C** $(5 \times 20) + 103$
B $(103 \div 5) - 20$ **D** $103 - 5 + 20$

8. The inputs, I, are 88, 77, 66, 55, and 44. The outputs, O, are 8, 7, 6, 5, and 4. Which shows the rule in equation form?

F $I - 11 = O$ **H** $I \div 11 = O$
G $11 \div I = O$ **J** $I \times 11 = O$

9. Write About It Explain how you arrived at your answer for Problem 8.

Possible answer: I looked for an operation on 88 that gives a value of 8 and thought "divide by 11." I tested my prediction on all the other inputs and outputs.

Mental Math: Multiplication Patterns

Write the correct answer.

1. What is the first step in finding the value of $12 - (8 + 3)$?

   _____ adding 8 + 3 _____

2. There are 40 coins in each roll of quarters. How many coins are in 8 rolls?

   _____ 320 coins _____

3. Nina's number machine changes one number into another. It changes the number 3 into the number 27, 10 into 90, and 12 into 108. What rule does the machine use?

   _____ Multiply by 9 _____

4. What basic fact is used to find the product 6×700? What is the product?

   _____ 6 × 7; 4,200 _____

Choose the letter of the correct answer.

5. Use a basic fact and a pattern to determine which of these is the product 3×900.

   A 27   C 2,700
   B 270   D 27,000

6. How many seconds are there in 4 minutes?

   F 60   H 240
   G 120   J 400

7. Which type of graph makes it easiest to find the median of a set of data?

   A Bar graph
   B Line graph
   C Stem-and-leaf plot
   D Double-bar graph

8. Liang mails some cassette tapes to his cousin. He packs his tapes in 3 boxes of 8 tapes each. He also puts 6 tapes in a bag. Which expression matches this?

   F $(3 \times 8) + 6$ H $6 - (3 \times 8)$
   G $5 \times (6 - 3)$ J $(5 + 6) + 3$

9. **Write About It**   Describe the steps you took to solve Problem 2.

   _____ I found 40 × 8 by finding 4 × 8 and adding one more zero in the _____

   _____ product, giving me 320. _____

Estimate Products

Understand ➡ Plan ➡ Solve ➡ Check

Write the correct answer.

1. A project that took 5 hours and 17 minutes was finished at 3:30 P.M. When was the project started?

10:13 A.M.

2. Eric estimates the product 7 × 428 to be 2,800. What basic fact did he use to arrive at this estimate?

7 × 4 = 28

3. What is the value of the digit 6 in the number 164,012?

60,000

4. Each of the 12 months has about 30 days. About how many days are in the year?

360

Choose the letter of the correct answer.

5. One mile of highway has 264 center lines. Which of the following basic math facts would be used to estimate the number of highway center lines in 9 miles of highway?

A 3 × 7 = 21   **C** 9 × 6 = 54
B 4 × 2 = 8   **D** 3 × 9 = 27

6. What type of graph is shown?

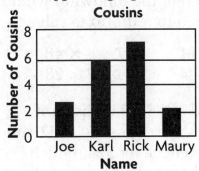

F Line plot
G Stem-and-leaf
H Bar graph
J Double-bar graph

7. Which of the following is a good estimate for the product 279 × 8?

A 20   **C** 2,400
B 24   **D** 24,000

8. School starts at 7:30 A.M. Students have three 1-hour classes and one 30-minute study period before lunch. When is lunch?

F 12:00 P.M.   **H** 11:30 A.M.
G 12:00 A.M.   **J** 11:00 A.M.

9. Write About It List the steps you took to solve Problem 7.

Possible answer: I rounded 279 to 300 and used the basic fact, 3 × 8 = 24. I wrote two zeros to get 2,400.

Multiply 2-Digit Numbers

Understand → Plan → Solve → Check

Write the correct answer.

1. Find the product. You may wish to use base-ten blocks.

$$3 \times 96$$

288

2. Find the product. You may wish to use base-ten blocks.

$$8 \times 69$$

552

3. Amanda works 18 hours each week for $7 an hour. How much does she earn each week?

$126

4. Nine people walk 14 miles each week. How many total miles do they walk?

126 miles

Choose the letter of the correct answer.

5. In which of the following would you need to regroup to solve?

A 9×11 **C** 4×48
B 2×34 D 3×23

6. What number times itself equals 81?

F 6   H 8
G 7   **J** 9

7. Richard has $269 in his bank account. He deposited $132 and wrote a check for $24. Which shows how to find how much money he has in his account now?

A $269 − $132 + $24
B $269 + $132 + $24
C $269 − $132 − $24
D $269 + $132 − $24

8. A concert starts at 8:00 P.M. Aldrece took a 75-minute bus ride to get to the concert. What time did Aldrece catch the bus to get to the concert?

F 7:05 P.M.   H 6:55 P.M.
G 7:10 P.M.   **J** 6:45 P.M.

9. **Write About It** Tell how you solved Problem 7.

Possible answer: A deposit is an addition and a check is a subtraction.

_____

_____

_____

Multiply 3- and 4-Digit Numbers

Understand ➡ Plan ➡ Solve ➡ Check

Write the correct answer.

1. A charity is hoping to raise
   $250,000. So far it has raised
   $178,260. How much more
   money does it need to raise
   to meet its goal?

   _____$71,740_____

2. A pilot flies 372 miles. She flies
   this same route 6 times. How
   many miles does she fly
   altogether?

   _____2,232 miles_____

3. Find the product of 4 × 2,165.
   Then estimate to check.

   _____8,660_____

4. Bryce has 56 trading cards. He
   puts 8 cards on each page of
   his collector's book. How many
   pages does he fill?

   _____7 pages_____

Choose the letter of the correct answer.

5. Which of the following numbers
   is the greatest?

   A 20,053
   B 23,500
   (**C**) 25,030
   D 25,003

6. Find the product of 5 × 347.

   F 352
   G 1,505
   H 1,535
   (**J**) 1,735

7. Which of the following is
   seventeen thousand, ten in
   standard form?

   (**A**) 17,010
   B 170,010
   C 17,001
   D 170,100

8. There are 3 jars of beads. Each jar
   has 472 beads. How many beads
   are there altogether?

   F 475 beads
   G 1,216 beads
   (**H**) 1,416 beads
   J 2,216 beads

9. **Write About It** How did you choose your answer to Problem 8?

   Possible answer: I found the product of 3 × 472 to find the total number

   of beads.

Multiply with Zeros

Write the correct answer.

1. Soccer practice started at
3:45 P.M. It ended at 5:10 P.M.
How long was soccer practice?

_____1 hr 25 min_____

2. There are 1,080 people at each
concert. If there are 3 concerts,
how many people see the concert
in all?

_____3,240 people_____

3. Find the product of 4 × 4,006.
Then estimate to check.

_____16,024_____

4. Carlos buys two magazines that
cost $3.75 each and a book that
costs $8.95. How much does he
spend in all?

_____$16.45_____

Choose the letter of the correct answer.

5. What is the expanded form of
5,032?

A 5,000 + 300 + 20
B 5,000 + 300 + 2
C 5,000 + 30 + 2
D 500 + 30 + 2

6. Find the product of 8 × 703.

F 5,624
G 5,604
H 711
J 584

7. Which of the following is the best
estimate of 7 × 208?

A 2,100   C 210
B 1,400   D 140

8. Mandy earns $20.50 for each tour
she guides. If she guides 3 tours,
how much does she earn
altogether?

F $60.15   H $61.15
G $60.50   J $61.50

9. **Write About It**   How did you choose your answer to Problem 8?

   Possible answer: I found the product of 3 × $20.50 to find the total

   amount.

© Harcourt

Name _____

Classify and Categorize

Understand ➡ Plan ➡ Solve ➡ Check

When you read a problem, it is often helpful to see if you can **classify** the information in the problem into categories. The things in a **category** have something in common, such as operations: addition, subtraction, multiplication, or division. As you read, look for words and phrases that are clues to which operation you can use.

VOCABULARY

classify
category

CATEGORIES			
ADDITION	**SUBTRACTION**	**MULTIPLICATION**	**DIVISION**
in all	more than	in all groups	in 1 group

Underline the words that help you categorize the information.

Daisy is the class treasurer. She needs to give $50 to each of four class committees. There is $300 in the class treasury. How much money will be in the treasury after Daisy gives out the money?

1. Write some other words that give clues about each category of problems. Possible answers given.

   Addition Problems _altogether, and, total_

   Subtraction Problems _less than, fewer than, difference, compare, take away_

   Multiplication Problems _total of groups_

   Division Problems _equal groups, in each group_

2. Solve the problem. In which category or categories—addition, subtraction, multiplication, or division—does this problem fit?

   300 − (4 × 50). There will be $100 left; multiplication and subtraction

3. Describe the problem solving strategy used. _I wrote an equation._

Name the category. Solve.

4. Mike went to the grocery store to buy fruit. He bought mangos for $2.76 and a sack of oranges for $4.89. How much money did he spend in all?

   addition problem;

   He spent $7.65.

5. Amber's mother gives her $4.75 each week for an allowance. Amber plans to save all of her allowance for 6 weeks. How much money will she have saved?

   multiplication problem;

   She will have saved $28.50.

Mental Math: Multiplication Patterns

Write the correct answer.

1. Use a basic fact and a pattern to find the products.

$$4 \times 70 = \underline{\ ?\ }$$
$$40 \times 70 = \underline{\ ?\ }$$
$$40 \times 700 = \underline{\ ?\ }$$

280; 2,800; 28,000

2. Solve.

$$\begin{array}{r} 800 \\ \times\ 60 \\ \hline \end{array}$$

48,000

3. Hal takes 8 rolls of dimes to the bank. Each roll holds $5 in dimes. How many $20 bills should the bank give Hal for his rolls of dimes?

two $20 bills

4. Carla's favorite piece of music is 17 minutes long. She likes to play it over and over again. About how long does it take her to listen to it 9 times?

about 180 min, or 3 hr

Choose the letter of the correct answer.

5. Which number will complete the pattern?

$$6 \times 90 = 540$$
$$60 \times 90 = 5,400$$
$$60 \times \underline{\ ?\ } = 54,000$$

A 9 B 90 C 900 D 9,000

6. Which product completes the number sentence?

$$50 \times 7,000 = \underline{\ ?\ }$$

F 3,500   H 42,000
G 35,000   J 350,000

7. Which type of graph best compares data for two similar groups?

A Double-bar graph
B Line Graph
C Stem-and-Leaf Plot
D Line Plot

8. Six partners agree to start a business together. Each partner will contribute $4,000 toward the business. The business will also take out a $15,000 loan. How much money will the business have?

F $19,000   H $39,000
G $24,000   J $45,000

9. **Write About It** Describe the pattern that you could use to solve Problem 6.

Possible answer: First find the basic fact product: $5 \times 7 = 35$; then count

the zeros in the factors $(1 + 3 = 4)$. Write the product with the

same number of zeros that are in the 2 factors; 350,000.

© Harcourt

Name _____

The Distributive Property

Understand ➡ Plan ➡ Solve ➡ Check

Write the correct answer.

1. Make a model and use the Distributive Property to find 8 × 24.

_____192_____

2. Alissa wants to walk 18 miles. She plans to walk the same number of miles each day for 6 days. How many miles should she walk each day?

_____3 miles_____

3. Pencils cost $0.25 each. Pens cost $0.50 each. How much will 2 pencils and 2 pens cost?

_____$1.50_____

4. Make a model and use the Distributive Property to find the product of 20 × 14.

___Check students' models; 280___

Choose the letter of the correct answer.

5. The program started at 2:50 P.M. It ended at 4:45 P.M. How long did the program last?

   A 1 hr 45 min
   B 1 hr 50 min
   C 1 hr 55 min
   D 2 hr 5 min

6. Which shows an example of the Distributive Property?

   F $(30 + 15) + 5 = 30 + (15 + 5)$
   G $30 × 15 = (30 × 10) + (30 × 5)$
   H $30 × (15 × 5) = (30 × 15) × 5$
   J $30 × (15 × 5) = 30 × (5 × 15)$

7. On Monday, Mr. Smithson drove 68 miles to the park entrance. Then he drove to the lake. He drove a total of 90 miles. How many miles was it to the lake?

   A 22 miles   **C** 158 miles
   B 32 miles   **D** 168 miles

8. Which property does the following demonstrate?

   $9 × 18 = (9 × 10) + (9 × 8)$

   F Zero Property
   G Commutative Property
   H Associative Property
   J Distributive Property

9. **Write About It** How did you choose your answer to Problem 8?

   Possible answer: The equation shows that multiplying a sum by a number
   is the same as multiplying each addend by the number and then adding
   the products. This is the Distributive Property.

Multiply by Tens

Write the correct answer.

Understand ➡ Plan ➡ Solve ➡ Check

1. Write the missing number to complete the pattern.

$$3 \times 50 = 150$$
$$3 \times 500 = 1,500$$
$$3 \times 5,000 = \underline{\ ?\ }$$

15,000

2. Write the missing number to complete the pattern.

$$5 \times 90 = 450$$
$$5 \times 900 = 4,500$$
$$5 \times \underline{\ ?\ } = 45,000$$

9,000

3. Find the product.

$$43 \times 60$$

2,580

4. Find the product.

$$32 \times 40$$

1,280

Choose the letter of the correct answer.

5. What number completes the multiplication sentence?

$$21 \times \underline{\ ?\ } = 1,260$$

A 9,000   **B** 900   **C** 600   **(D)** 60

6. What number completes the multiplication sentence?

$$32 \times \underline{\ ?\ } = 2,880$$

F 60   **G** 70   **H** 80   **(J)** 90

7. Ralph goes to the movies with a friend. He buys 2 tickets for $7.50 each. He also buys a $3.50 bucket of popcorn and a $2.25 cup of soda. He has $3.50 left when he gets home. How much did he have when he went to the movies?

A $25.75   **C** $19.50
(B) $24.25   **D** $16.75

8. Lila puts the coins from her coin jar into rolls. She has 9 rolls of quarters. Each roll holds 40 quarters. She has 7 rolls of nickels. Each roll holds 40 nickels. What is the total value of her rolls of coins?

F $36   **(H)** $104
G $44   **J** $640

9. **Write About It** Describe the strategy you used to solve Problem 8.

Possible answer: There are 4 quarters in $1, so 40 quarters are equal to

$10; $10 × 9 rolls = $90; 40 nickels = 40 × 5 cents = 200 cents, or $2;

$2 × 7 rolls = $14; $90 + $14 = $104.

Estimate Products

Write the correct answer.

1. Round each factor to its greatest place value, and then estimate the product.

$$\begin{array}{r} 56 \\ \times\ 34 \\ \hline \end{array}$$

1,800

2. Round each factor to its greatest place value, and then estimate the product.

$$\begin{array}{r} 481 \\ \times\ 18 \\ \hline \end{array}$$

10,000

3. The Rocky Glen Amusement Park is open for 70 days during the summer. About 800 children visit the park every day. About how many children visit the park during the summer?

about 56,000 children

4. The Rocky Glen Amusement Park has a roller coaster which has 32 seats. Write an expression for the number of riders in some number of trips, t.

$32 \times t$

Choose the letter of the correct answer.

5. Which is the most reasonable estimate of the product?

$$\begin{array}{r} 166 \\ \times\ 84 \\ \hline \end{array}$$

A 16,000   **C** 7,200
B 9,000   **D** 1,600

6. Which is the most reasonable estimate of the product?

28×910

F 27,000   **H** 2,700
G 18,000   **J** 1,800

7. Mike places some tiles in an array that is 5 tiles long by 7 tiles wide. He has 7 more tiles in a pile. How many tiles does Mike have altogether?

A 19
B 28
C 42
D 54

8. There are 276 students at Norris Elementary. The cafeteria manager estimates that each student uses about 28 napkins each month at lunch. Which box of napkins should she order for next month?

F the 500-napkin box
G the 1,000-napkin box
H the 10,000-napkin box
J the 20,000-napkin box

9. **Write About It** Explain how you chose your answer to Problem 7.

Possible answer: I drew a 5 by 7 array and counted that it had 35 tiles.

To find the total number of tiles, I added 7 to 35 and got 42.

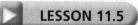

Cause and Effect

Understand ➤ Plan ➤ Solve ➤ Check

Sometimes the information in a problem is related. The **cause** is the reason something happened. The **effect** is the result.

Read the following problem.

Rita needs to make programs to hand out at the school play. She needs one program per seat. There are 34 rows of seats and 20 seats in each row. How many programs does Rita need to make?

1. List the causes in the **CAUSE** column.
   List the effects in the **EFFECT** column. Possible responses:

CAUSE	EFFECT
Programs are needed for the school play.	Rita will make programs.
There needs to be one program per seat.	Rita needs to find out how many programs to make.

2. Solve the problem. $(30 \times 20) + (4 \times 20) = 680$; Rita needs to make

   680 programs.

3. Describe the strategy you used. I looked for causes and effects to help

   understand the problem. Then I solved a simpler problem by breaking

List a cause and effect in each problem. Solve. 34 into parts that are easier to
   multiply.

4. Juan built a fence to keep his dog in the yard. Each fence section cost $25. He used 20 sections. How much money did the fence cost?

   Possible cause: Juan needed to

   keep his dog in the yard.

   Possible effect: Juan built a

   fence. $500

5. To prepare for a predicted snow storm, Jean needs to have on hand 10 bottles of water for each of her 123 hotel guests. How many bottles of water does Jean need?

   Possible cause: Storm is

   predicted. Possible effect: Jean

   needs to get bottles of water.

   1,230 bottles of water

© Harcourt

Multiply 2-Digit Numbers

Understand → Plan → Solve → Check

Write the correct answer.

1.
$$\begin{array}{r} 74 \\ \times\ 23 \\ \hline 1{,}702 \end{array}$$

2.
$$36 \times 48$$

1,728

3. Each bag holds 18 oranges. A store gets a shipment of 42 bags of oranges. How many oranges are in the shipment?

756 oranges

4. If a school bus can carry 25 students, how many students can 40 buses carry?

1,000 students

Choose the letter of the correct answer.

5. 87×44

  A 348,348   C 3,848
  B 4,268   D 3,828

6. What is the most reasonable estimate of 78×78?

  F About 64,000   H About 6,400
  G About 49,000   J About 640

7. A *pica* is a unit of measure used by book designers. A page in a book of poems has 1 line of text per pica. There are 26 lines of text on the page. The top and bottom margins of the page are each 6 picas. How many picas high is the page?

  A 54   C 38
  B 46   D 26

8. There are 36 inches in 1 yard. How many inches are there in 15 yards?

  F 1,296 inches
  G 540 inches
  H 510 inches
  J 410 inches

9. **Write About It** Describe how you found the number of inches in 15 yards in Problem 8.

Possible answer: 1 yard has 36 inches, so 15 yards has (15 × 36) inches.

15 × 36 = 540.

Multiply 3-Digit Numbers

Write the correct answer.

1.

$$\begin{array}{r} 711 \\ \times\ \ 55 \\ \hline \end{array}$$

_39,105_

2.

$$39 \times \$237$$

_\$9,243_

3. Suppose your heart beats about 67 times per minute. Estimate the number of times it beats in 1 hour.

about 4,200 times

4. Judy changes the oil in her car every 5,000 miles. She has changed the oil a total of 12 times since she bought the car. How many miles has the car been driven?

60,000 miles

Choose the letter of the correct answer.

5. $77 \times \$830$

  A $58,158   **C** $65,510

  B $63,910   **D** $67,810

6. 64×371

  F 24,544   **H** 23,644

  G 23,744   **J** 23,544

7. Doug's Pet Shop sells ultrasonic flea collars for $49.95. Over the past year, it has sold 93 of the collars. How much money has the shop received from the sale of the flea collars?

  A $5,196.20   **C** $4,842.30

  B $4,645.35   **D** $3,679.25

8. The moon is full about every 29 days. About how many full moons will there be in a 90-day period starting after the next full moon?

  F 9

  G 4

  H 3

  J 2

9. Write About It Explain how you found the answer to Problem 8.

Possible answer: I rounded 29 to 30. To find how many full moons in a

90-day period, I used a basic fact and a pattern. 30 × 3 = 90.

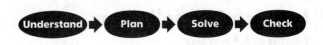
Choose a Method

Write the correct answer.

1.

$$\begin{array}{r} 2{,}162 \\ \times\ 32 \\ \hline \end{array}$$

69,184

2.

$$\begin{array}{r} 8{,}543 \\ \times\ 29 \\ \hline \end{array}$$

247,747

3. The New Bedford Soccer League has 6 teams. Each team has 13 players. How many players are there in the New Bedford Soccer League?

78 players

4. The Century Scholarship Fund gives out 18 scholarships each year. If each of the scholarships is worth $2,500, how much money does the fund give out each year?

$45,000

Choose the letter of the correct answer.

5. $11 \times \$2{,}113$

A $23,243
B $22,243

C $21,130
D $4,226

6.

$$\begin{array}{r} 4{,}132 \\ \times\ 16 \\ \hline \end{array}$$

F 65,012
G 65,021

H 66,021
J 66,112

7. Eileen is a marathon runner. Each weekday, she runs 13 miles. Each Saturday and Sunday, she runs 17 miles. How much farther does she run in all during the 5 weekdays than she runs on Saturday and Sunday?

A 99 mi
B 65 mi

C 55 mi
D 31 mi

8. Each time Chris shovels Mrs. Barr's driveway after it snows, Mrs. Barr deposits $9 into Chris's college tuition fund. During the winter, it snowed 27 times. How much money did Mrs. Barr deposit into Chris's college tuition fund?

F $270
G $253

H $243
J $234

9. Write About It Describe the steps you took to solve Problem 7.

Possible answer: First I multiplied 13 miles × 5 days: 3 × 5 = 15, 5 × 10 = 50,

50 + 15 = 65; then I multiplied 17 miles × 2 days: 2 × 7 = 14, 2 × 10 = 20,

20 + 14 = 34; finally, I subtracted: 65 miles − 34 miles = 31 miles.

Practice Multiplication Using Money

Understand ➡ Plan ➡ Solve ➡ Check

Write the correct answer.

1. Solve.

$$35 \times \$2.77$$

$\underline{\hspace{4em}\$96.95\hspace{4em}}$

2. Solve.

$$\begin{array}{r} \$76.44 \\ \times \quad 24 \\ \hline \end{array}$$

$\underline{\hspace{4em}\$1,834.56\hspace{4em}}$

3. Nathan decides to write a book about his experiences in fourth grade. He plans to write at least 250 words each day. After 5 days of writing, what is the least number of words he should have?

$\underline{\hspace{3em}1,250\ words\hspace{3em}}$

4. Maura reads that there are an average of 3 radios for every person in the country. She lives in a town of about 7,000 people. About how many radios can she expect there to be in her town?

$\underline{\hspace{2em}about\ 21,000\ radios\hspace{2em}}$

Choose the letter of the correct answer.

5.
$$\begin{array}{r} \$6,543 \\ \times \quad 42 \\ \hline \end{array}$$

A $298,805   **C** $219,485

B $274,806   **D** $219,480

6. Which number completes the pattern?

$$8 \times 40 = 320$$
$$8 \times \underline{\ ?\ } = 3,200$$
$$8 \times 4,000 = 32,000$$

F 4   **G** 40   **H** 400   **J** 4,000

7. Ellen builds an electric motor from a kit. She winds 500 turns of wire in a coil to make an electromagnet. She estimates there are about 2 inches of wire in each turn. About how many inches of wire did she use?

A 750 in.   **C** 1,000 in.

B 900 in.   **D** 1,100 in.

8. Liang moves to a new home. He packs his tapes in 3 boxes of 8 tapes each. He also puts 6 tapes in a bag. Which expression can you use to find out how many tapes Liang owns?

F $(3 \times 8) + 6$ **H** $(5 \times 6) - 3$

G $(6 - 3) \times 8$ **J** $3 \times (8 + 6)$

9. Write About It Describe the steps you took to solve Problem 7.

Possible answer: If there is about 2 in. in each of 500 turns, then there

is about 1,000 in. of wire. I multiplied 500 × 2.

© Harcourt

Use Context Clues

Understand ➡ Plan ➡ Solve ➡ Check

Words or phrases in a problem can help you understand the meaning and the mathematical operations you must perform. Read the following problem.

Julia has $45.00 to spend at the party store. She selects 16 favors, which cost $1.29 each. Then she finds 32 balloons, which cost $0.59 each. Then she selects 2 packs of paper plates, which cost $1.79 per pack, and 1 pack of napkins which costs $1.89. How much money will her purchases cost? Does she have enough money to buy everything?

1. Underline the context clues to help you decide whether you need to give an exact answer or an estimated answer to each question in the problem. Then explain what the context clues tell you.

Context Clues	**Explanation**
How much money will her purchases cost?	"How much" means find the exact amount.
Does she have enough money to buy everything?	"Does she have enough" means you need to find a total and compare it.

2. Solve each part of the problem.

$16 \times \$1.29 = \$20.64; 32 \times \$0.59 = \$18.88; 2 \times \$1.79 = 3.58; 1 \times \$1.89 = \$1.89; \$20.64 + \$18.88 + \$3.58 + \$1.89 = \$44.99; \$44.99 < \$45.00$, so Julia has enough money.

Underline the context clues. Solve the problem.

3. The club has $63.85 in its treasury. There are 23 new members and they must pay $2.50 each to join the club. How much money will the club have then?

$121.35

4. A one-way bus trip from Atlanta to Tallahassee costs $45. Mr. Jones has $150. Does he have enough money for 2 tickets from Atlanta to Tallahassee and back? Explain.

No, $90 \times 2 = \$180; \$180 > \$150$

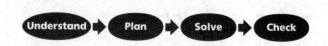
Divide with Remainders

Write the correct answer.

1. Mrs. Wong is giving her teacup collection to her 9 grandchildren. She has 67 teacups. What is the greatest number of teacups she can give to each grandchild?

_____ 7 teacups _____

2. In problem 1, how many teacups will be left over?

_____ 4 teacups _____

3. Roy is painting his house. He rents a paint sprayer for $29.95 a day. It takes him 13 days to paint the house. Write his total cost for renting the sprayer.

_____ $389.35 _____

4. Jeanna and Crystal take an 8-day bike trip. They bike 60 miles each day. Do they bike more than 500 miles? Explain.

_____ No, because 60 × 8 = 480 _____

Choose the letter of the correct answer.

5. 7)‾43‾

   A 5 r7   **C** 6 r1
   B 6   **D** 6 r4

6. 5)‾38‾

   F 6 r8   **H** 7 r5
   G 7 r3   **J** 8 r2

7. A typical baby wears about 5 diapers a day for the first 2 years of life. About how many diapers does the baby need?

   A 2,000
   B 3,000
   C 4,000
   D 7,000

8. Earth's diameter is about 7,900 miles. The distance from Earth to the moon is about 30 times this diameter. Estimate the distance from Earth to the moon.

   F about 21,000 mi
   G about 31,000 mi
   H about 240,000 mi
   J about 310,000 mi

9. Write About It Describe the method you used to solve Problem 7.

_____ Possible answer: First I found the number of days in 2 years by _____

_____ multiplying 2 × 365; Then I multiplied that product by 5 diapers a day. _____

Model Division

Write the correct answer.

Understand ➡ Plan ➡ Solve ➡ Check

1. What division problem is modeled by the following?

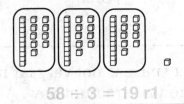

_____ 58 ÷ 3 = 19 r1 _____

2. Theresa's state sales tax requires her to pay 6 cents for each dollar she spends. If she buys a dog collar for $4.00 and a leash for $7.00, how much sales tax will she pay?

_____ 66 cents, or $0.66 _____

3. Make or draw a model to solve.

34 ÷ 7

_____ 4 r6 _____

4. Make or draw a model to solve.

87 ÷ 6

_____ 14 r3 _____

Choose the letter of the correct answer.

5. 67 ÷ 5

A 13 r1   **C** 13 r3
B 13 r2   **D** 13 r4

6. What division problem is shown?

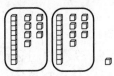

F 35 ÷ 2 = 17 r1 **H** 35 ÷ 1 = 17 r1
G 34 ÷ 2 = 17 r1 **J** 35 ÷ 17 = 17 r1

7. The Band Boosters are selling T-shirts. Each T-shirt costs $5 to make and is sold for $11. The Band Boosters ordered 300 shirts and have sold 250. How much money have they made?

A $250   **C** $1,500
B $1,250   **D** $2,750

8. Write an equation using a variable: 68 cars in 4 rows is some number of cars in each row.

F 68 + 4 = b   **H** 68 × 4 = b
G 68 − 4 = b   **J** 68 ÷ 4 = b

9. **Write About It** Explain your solution to Problem 7.

Possible answer: I multiplied $5 × 300 to find the amount paid for the

T-shirts. Then I multiplied $11 × 250 to find the amount made on the sale

of T-shirts. The difference ($2,750 − $1,500 = $1,250) is the amount of

money made.

Name _____

Division Procedures

Write the correct answer.

Understand → Plan → Solve → Check

1. Solve.

   $7)\overline{94}$

   13 r3

2. Solve.

   $3)\overline{98}$

   32 r2

3. Mr. Butterfield bakes a batch of 48 cookies for his 5 children. If each child gets the same number of cookies, how many will be left over?

   3 cookies

4. Outer space is not very far from where you are right now. At a speed of 60 miles per hour, you could travel out of the Earth's atmosphere in about 10 hours. Estimate this distance.

   about 600 mi

Choose the letter of the correct answer.

5. $6)\overline{75}$

   A 12 r2   **C** 12 r5
   B 12 r3   **D** 12

6. $4)\overline{89}$

   F 22 r1   **H** 23
   G 22 r3   **J** 42 r1

7. Jerry had 64 baseball cards. He gave half to Craig. Craig gave half of his cards to Steve. How many cards did Craig give Steve?

   A 16 cards
   B 18 cards
   C 32 cards
   D 48 cards

8. The principal wants to invite the 3 fourth-grade classes to a party. Two classes have 27 students each, and the third class has 18 students. How many tables are needed to seat 8 students at each table?

   F 6 tables   **H** 8 tables
   G 7 tables   **J** 9 tables

9. **Write About It** Explain how you estimated the first digit of the quotient in Problem 6.

   Possible answer: Since there are enough tens to place the first digit of

   the quotient in the tens place, I estimated 80 ÷ 4 = 20.

© Harcourt

Name _____

Analyze Information

Understand ➡ Plan ➡ Solve ➡ Check

It is helpful to **analyze,** or examine, the details in a problem. You can then use the details to solve the problem. Underline the details so you will remember them. Read the following problem.

VOCABULARY
analyze

> Mary Lou's parents saved money for a piano that cost $1,845. They made a down payment of $1,215. They paid off the remaining amount in 9 months, paying the same amount every month. What was their monthly payment?

1. Analyze each detail of the problem. Complete the sentence in the **Explanation** column of the table for each detail.

Detail	Explanation
The piano cost $1,845.	The total cost was _$1,845_.
They paid $1,215 down payment.	Subtract _$1,215_ from _$1,845_.
They paid the rest in 9 equal payments.	Divide _$630_ by _9_.

2. Solve the problem.

$1,845 − $1,215 = $630; $630 ÷ 9 = $70; Their monthly payment was $70.

3. Describe the strategy you used. Possible answer: I wrote number

sentences.

Underline the details. Write a number sentence to solve.

4. It costs the press club $81.73 to print each issue of their newspaper, *School Scoop*. If they print 6 issues of the paper during the year, how much money will they spend?

6 × $81.73 = $490.38

5. Kyla saved $108.60 in the bank in one year. She earned $7.24 in interest on the money in the bank. Kyla then took out $47.25 to buy a camera. How much did she have left in the bank?

$108.60 + $7.24 − $47.25 =

$68.59

Name _____

Mental Math: Division Patterns

Understand ➡ Plan ➡ Solve ➡ Check

Write the correct answer.

1. Write the number to finish the pattern.

$$240 \div 6 = 40$$
$$2,400 \div 6 = 400$$
$$24,000 \div 6 = \underline{\ ?\ }$$

_____4,000_____

2. Four friends play a game with a deck of 52 cards. The players divide all of the cards equally. Write the number of cards each player gets.

_____13 cards_____

3. Use a basic fact and patterns to find the quotient.

$$5,400 \div 6$$

_____900_____

4. Renee has 76 quarters. Write the value of her quarters in dollars.

_____$19.00_____

Choose the letter of the correct answer.

5. What is the most reasonable estimate of the quotient?

$4,178 \div 5$

A 250   **B** 600   **C** 800   **D** 700

6. $63,000 \div 7$

F 800   **G** 900   **H** 7,000   **J** 9,000

7. Chesterton was hit with a huge snowstorm that left an average of 2 inches of snow each hour. The storm left a total of 2 feet of snow. How long did the storm last?

A 12 hr
B 18 hr
C 24 hr
D 36 hr

8. A train leaves Station 1 at 8:15 A.M. It travels east for 45 minutes and stops at Station 2 for 30 minutes before leaving again. At what times does the train leave Station 2?

F 8:45 A.M.
G 9:15 A.M.
H 9:30 A.M.
J 9:45 A.M.

9. Write About It Describe the steps you took to solve Problem 7.

Possible answer: I changed 2 ft into 24 in. Then I divided 24 in. by 2 in.

each hour to find the length of the storm, or 12 hr.

© Harcourt

PS70   Problem Solving

Estimate Quotients

Understand ➡ Plan ➡ Solve ➡ Check

Write the correct answer.

1. Write an estimate of the quotient by using compatible numbers.

$$522 \div 6 = \underline{\ ?\ }$$

Possible answer: 90

2. Write a pair of compatible numbers. Use them to estimate the quotient.

$$8\overline{)6{,}321}$$

Possible answers: $6{,}400 \div 8 = 800$, $5{,}600 \div 8 = 700$

3. Koala Airlines carries an average of 272 passengers on its Dallas to Perth flight. It runs 620 of these flights each year. About how many passengers travel from Dallas to Perth each year?

About 180,000 passengers

4. Chester runs his horses in an eight-sided pen. Each of the pen's sides measures 240 ft. What is the distance around the pen?

1,920 ft

Choose the letter of the correct answer.

5. Which expression would be best to estimate the quotient?

$$312 \div 6 = \underline{\ ?\ }$$

A 300 ÷ 6   C 310 ÷ 6
B 290 ÷ 6   D 320 ÷ 6

6. Which is the most reasonable estimate of the quotient?

$$5{,}549 \div 8 = \underline{\ ?\ }$$

F 700   G 80   H 75   J 70

7. A group of 12 friends buys 125 concert tickets. Which of the following is not a way the tickets can be split?

A Each friend gets 11 tickets.
B Each friend gets 10; 5 are returned.
C Seven friends get 10; 5 friends get 11.
D Five friends get 18; 7 friends get 5.

8. Bart wrote his name 53 times in 266 seconds. About how long does it take him to write his name each time?

F about 10 sec
G about 8 sec
H about 5 sec
J about 3 sec

9. **Write About It**   Explain how you chose compatible numbers to estimate the quotient in Problem 2.   Possible answer:

I looked for a multiple of 8 that was close to the dividend. 6,400 is close to

6,321, so I used the basic fact $64 \div 8 = 8$ to find $6{,}400 \div 8 = 800$.

Place the First Digit

Write the correct answer.

Understand ➡ Plan ➡ Solve ➡ Check

1. Tell where to place the first digit of the quotient.

$$4\overline{)965}$$

hundreds place
_____

2. Divide.

$$6\overline{)822}$$

137
_____

3. Find the mode: 3, 7, 4, 9, 4, 2, 3, 4, 6, 9.

4
_____

4. When the BookPort has its books on sale for $9.99 each, Penny buys 8 books. How much do the 8 books cost her?

$79.92
_____

Choose the letter of the correct answer.

5. $5\overline{)676}$

A 225 r1   **C** 125 r1
B 135 r1   **D** 115 r1

6. $7\overline{)449}$

F 64 r5   **H** 64 r1
G 64 r3   **J** 64

7. Sam plans to see a 97-minute movie at the twin theater. The movie starts at 7:45 P.M. After that he wants to see the other movie the theater is showing. Which is the earliest time the other movie could start for Sam to be able to see both movies?

A 9:05 P.M.   **C** 9:45 P.M.
B 9:15 P.M.   **D** 10:35 P.M.

8. To find her math grade, Edna adds up all 7 of her test scores and then divides that sum by 7. What is Edna's average grade?

Test	1	2	3	4	5	6	7
Score	92	82	76	88	95	71	98

F 86   **H** 88
G 87   **J** 92

9. Write About It Explain how you solved Problem 7.

Possible answer: I found the time that the first movie would end by adding

the length of the first movie (97 minutes) and the starting time (7:45 P.M.):

9:22 P.M.: then I compared 9:22 P.M. to the answer choices. The earliest

time after 9:22 P.M. is 9:45 P.M.

Divide 3-Digit Numbers

Understand ➡ Plan ➡ Solve ➡ Check

Write the correct answer.

1. Divide.

$$4\overline{)871}$$

217 r3

2. Divide.

$$3\overline{)555}$$

185

3. Heidi spends $2.10 each on a strip of 4 Priority Mail stamps. How much did she spend altogether?

$8.40

4. Sheldon's dog had to spend 12 days in a veterinary hospital. The cost was $98 each day. How much was the total hospital bill?

$1,176

Choose the letter of the correct answer.

5. $6\overline{)458}$

A 76 r2   **C** 78 r4

B 78 r2   **D** 79 r4

6. $5\overline{)911}$

F 168 r1   **H** 182 r1

G 178 r1   **J** 190 r1

7. While flipping through the calendar in his date book, Matt sees this pattern: 31, 28, 31, 30, 31, 30, 31, ... Which is the next number in the pattern?

A 31

B 30

C 29

D 28

8. Raul drives his car to work and back 5 days each week. His business is 7 miles from his home. On Saturdays, he drives to the mall, which is 12 miles from his home. How many miles does Raul drive each year?

F 6,512 mi   **H** 3,888 mi

G 4,888 mi   **J** 3,360 mi

9. Write About It Explain the pattern you found in Problem 7.

Possible answer: The pattern is the number of days in the months of the

calendar, starting with January. The next month in the pattern is August,

which has 31 days.

Name _____

Zeros in Division

Understand ➡ Plan ➡ Solve ➡ Check

Write the correct answer.

1. Solve.

$$8\overline{)875}$$

109 r3

_____

2. Solve.

$$6\overline{)\$9.60}$$

$1.60

_____

3. The fleshy hawthorn is a small tree. One of the tallest ones is only 8 feet tall. The tallest redwood is about 360 feet tall. About how many of the fleshy hawthorns would it take to equal the height of the 360-foot redwood?

about 45 hawthorns

_____

4. Coach Jared orders new uniforms for all 22 of the team members. If each uniform costs $38.85, how much will the uniforms cost altogether?

$854.70

_____

Choose the letter of the correct answer.

5. $7\overline{)764}$

  A 108   **C** 109 r4

  B 109 r1   **D** 111 r3

6. $4\overline{)\$8.28}$

  F $2.07   **G** 2.07   **H** 2.03   **J** $2.03

7. Byron divides $474.40 by 4. He writes his answer as 118.6. How should he have written it?

  A $118.6

  B 118.60

  C $118.60

  D $118.00

8. At Green's Grocery, detergent is selling at 3 bottles for $9.00. At O'Malley's, the same detergent is 5 bottles for $10.00. Which store has the better buy and how much would you save on each bottle?

  F Green's; save $3.00 per bottle

  G Green's; save $2.00 per bottle

  H O'Malley's; save $2.00 per bottle

  J O'Malley's; save $1.00 per bottle

9. Write About It Describe the steps you took to solve Problem 8.

Possible answer: I found the price per bottle at each store by dividing.

$9.00 ÷ 3 = $3.00; $10.00 ÷ 5 = $2.00. Then, subtracted to find the

difference.

Choose a Method

Write the correct answer.

1. Solve.

$$8)\overline{\$41.28}$$

$5.16

2. Solve.

$$9)\overline{3,771}$$

419

3. If an egg weighs about 45 grams, about how much will 1 dozen eggs weigh?

about 540 g

4. The Trueblue Theater holds 345 people. If it sold out every show during a 22-show run, how many people had tickets to the show?

7,590 people

Choose the letter of the correct answer.

5. $4)\overline{\$22.36}$

A $5.64
B $5.59

C $5.54
D $4.55

6. 997
$\times$ 37

F 32,449
G 36,209

H 36,889
J 38,989

7. Harriet wants to find the cost per pound of a 5-pound bag of potatoes that is labeled $7.85. She divides $7.85 by 5 and writes her answer as $157 per pound. How should she have written her answer?

A $157.00 per lb
B 157 per lb
C $15.70 per lb
D $1.57 per lb

8. Sweet corn is priced at 3 ears for $0.99. Shawna wants to buy 14 ears for a party. How much will the corn cost?

F $17.50
G $5.62
H $4.95
J $4.62

9. Write About It Explain how you solved Problem 8.

Possible answer: I first found the price per ear by dividing

$0.99 ÷ 3 = $0.33; Then I multiplied $0.33 × 14 = $4.62.

Use Graphic Aids

Understand ➤ Plan ➤ Solve ➤ Check

VOCABULARY
graphic aids

Graphic aids such as maps and diagrams give important information for solving problems. Read the following problem.

Josh is conducting a survey along Grove Street, beginning at 18 Grove Street, and surveying the buildings in numerical order. He has 90 minutes before meeting his friend. It takes him 8 minutes to survey each building. How many buildings can Josh survey before his meeting? Where should he tell his friend to meet him?

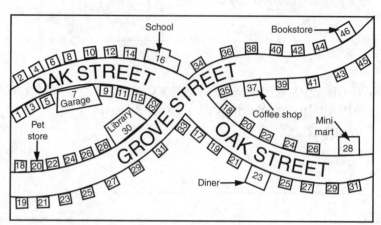

1. Use the map to help you solve the problem.

Divide to find the number of buildings Josh can survey before meeting his friend.	11 r 2
He can survey ___11___ buildings and meet his friend on time.	8)90 − 8 10 − 8 2
At what address will Josh be when he completes that number of surveys? _____28 Grove Street_____	

2. Solve the problem. 11 buildings; he can survey 11 buildings and have

   2 minutes left before meeting his friend; at the library.

3. Describe the strategy you used. Possible answer: I divided, and used the map.

Use the map to help you solve the problem.

4. Josh conducts a survey along Oak Street. It takes him 6 minutes for each building beginning at 1 Oak Street. He has 135 minutes before meeting his father. How many buildings can Josh survey? Explain how you know and tell where his father should meet him.

   22 buildings; he can survey 22 buildings and still have

   3 minutes before meeting his father, 135 ÷ 6 = 22 r3; at the diner.

Division Patterns to Estimate

Understand ➡ Plan ➡ Solve ➡ Check

Write the correct answer.

1. Round the divisor and the dividend. Estimate the quotient.

$$446 \div 93$$

$$450 \div 90 = 5$$

2. Round the divisor and the dividend. Estimate the quotient.

$$652 \div 77$$

$$640 \div 80 = 8$$

3. Write the basic fact you can use to help you estimate the quotient.

$$351 \div 6$$

$$36 \div 6 = 6$$

4. Divide.

$$267 \div 3$$

$$89$$

Choose the letter of the correct answer.

5. Which number will finish the pattern?

$$90 \div 30 = 3$$
$$900 \div 30 = 30$$
$$9,000 \div 30 = 300$$
$$90,000 \div 30 = \underline{\ ?\ }$$

   A 30,000   C 300
   B 3,000   D 30

6. Which number will finish the pattern?

$$20 \times 40 = 800$$
$$200 \times 40 = 8,000$$
$$2,000 \times 40 = 80,000$$
$$20,000 \times 40 = \underline{\ ?\ }$$

   F 800   H 80,000
   G 8,000   **J** 800,000

7. Ms. Felton makes $22 an hour as a consultant. How much did she earn during the week of January 19, 1998?

Hours Worked Week of Jan. 19, 1998

Day	Mon.	Tue.	Wed.	Thu.	Fri.	Sat.
Time	6 hr	8 hr	10 hr	9 hr	5 hr	6 hr

   A $360   C $898
   B $880   **D** $968

8. A theater company rents a stage for a total of 32 hours. They pay $296 for the space. Which is the most reasonable estimate of what they pay for the space each hour?

   F $18   **H** $10
   G $12   J $6

9. **Write About It** Describe the pattern you used to help you find the missing number in Problem 5.

Possible answer: First, find the basic fact quotient; then, subtract the number of zeros in the divisor from the number in the dividend; write that number of zeros in the quotient.

Model Division

Write the correct answer.

Understand ➡ Plan ➡ Solve ➡ Check

1. What division problem is shown by the model?

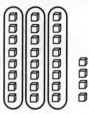

28 ÷ 8 = 3 r4

2. Jennifer is arranging flowers into bouquets. She has 258 flowers and needs to make 12 bouquets. About how many flowers will be in each bouquet?

about 20

3. Bailey's baby brother was born 128 days ago. If there are 7 days in each week, how many weeks ago was Bailey's baby brother born?

18 weeks, 2 days

4. Make a model to solve.

$$115 \div 36$$

Check students' models; 3 r7

Choose the letter of the correct answer.

5. Which division problem is shown by the model?

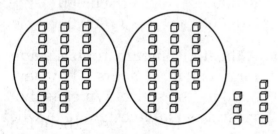

A 51 ÷ 22 = 2 r7
B 51 ÷ 2 = 22 r7
C 22 ÷ 7 = 51 r2
D 22 ÷ 2 = 51 r7

6. An Internet service provider runs 37 servers. Each server gets about 30,000 visits, or "hits," each day. Which is the most reasonable claim for the service provider to make?

F More than 500 hits a day!
G More than 1 million hits a day!
H More than 2 million hits a day!
J More than 5 million hits a day!

7. Divide. 834 ÷ 26

A 320   **C** 31 r2
B 32 r2   **D** 30 r2

8. Multiply. 21 × 6,518

F 136,878   **H** 126,878
G 136,778   **J** 126,778

9. Write About It Explain how you chose your answer for Problem 6.

Possible answer: I estimated 37 × 30,000 as 40 × 30,000

= 1,200,000. 1,200,000 > 1,000,000, so I chose G.

Division Procedures

Write the correct answer.

Understand → Plan → Solve → Check

1. Kim earned $578 in 34 weeks. If Kim earned the same amount each week, how much money did Kim earn in one week?

   $17

2. Jim earned $921 in one year, or 52 weeks. Did he earn more or less than $17 in one week?

   more

3. Jerry runs probability experiments on his computer. Each experiment takes 20 days to complete. What is the greatest number of experiments he can run in 1 year (365 days)?

   18 experiments

4. Lee completes a 985-mile car trip at an average speed of 52 miles per hour. About how many hours did she spend driving on the trip?

   about 20 hr

Choose the letter of the correct answer.

5. $28\overline{)656}$

   A 22 r16 C 23 r12
   B 22 r18 D 23 r2

6. $47\overline{)781}$

   F 12 r15 H 18 r2
   G 16 r29 J 19 r29

7. Tina slept 8, 9, 7, 10, 8, 8, and 9 hours the past 7 nights. What is the mode of the number of hours she slept?

   A 7 hours C 9 hours
   B 8 hours D 10 hours

8. Felicia's school has 427 students. There are 19 teachers. About how many students are in each class?

   F 30 H 20
   G 25 J 15

9. **Write About It** Describe how you answered Problem 4.

   Possible answer: I rounded 52 to 50; then rounded 985 to 1,000;

   1,000 ÷ 50 = 20 hours.

Correcting Quotients

Write the correct answer.

Understand ➡ Plan ➡ Solve ➡ Check

1. Write *too high*, *too low*, or *just right* to describe the estimated quotient.

$$\overset{9}{42)\overline{368}}$$

_____too high_____

2. Write *too high*, *too low*, or *just right* to describe the estimated quotient.

$$\overset{2}{77)\overline{231}}$$

_____too low_____

3. The wrestling team spent $375 buying sweatshirts for its 25 wrestlers. How much did each sweatshirt cost?

_____$15_____

4. The administrator who manages the school computers orders 36 copies of a software package. The total charge will be $972. What is the cost for a single copy?

_____$27_____

Choose the letter of the correct answer.

5. $71)\overline{365}$

  A 4 r10   **C** 6 r10
  B 5 r10   **D** 6 r61

6. $58)\overline{447}$

  F 5 r33   **H** 7 r41
  G 6 r45   **J** 8 r3

7. Ben takes 7 rolls of the same coins to the bank. Which choice *cannot* be the total value of the 7 coin rolls?

Coin	penny	nickel	dime	quarter
Number in roll	50	40	50	40

  A $3.50   **C** $14.00
  B $7.00   **D** $70.00

8. Brita has 372 dimes and 185 nickels. She puts the dimes in rolls of 50 per roll and the nickels in rolls of 40 per roll. How many rolls does she have?

  F 7 rolls of dimes, 3 rolls of nickels
  G 6 rolls of dimes, 4 rolls of nickels
  H 7 rolls of dimes, 4 rolls of nickels
  J 6 rolls of dimes, 3 rolls of nickels

9. **Write About It** Describe the steps you took to solve Problem 8.

Possible answer: First, I divided: 372 dimes ÷ 50 per roll = 7 rolls

with 22 left over; then, I divided 185 nickels ÷ 40 per roll = 4 rolls with 25

left over.

Name _____

Draw Conclusions

Understand ➡ Plan ➡ Solve ➡ Check

Draw conclusions is an important part of solving problems. To draw conclusions, you must examine the information in the problem and use what you already know to find the answer. Read the following problem.

VOCABULARY

draw conclusions

Carol practiced her flute for 360 minutes this week. Alberto practiced his flute for 7 hours. Who practiced longer?

1. Under *Examine the Information* complete the information that is given in the problem. In the next column, write some helpful information that you already know. Use this information to help you draw a conclusion.

Examine the Information	Use What You Already Know
• Carol practiced her flute for 360 min.	• There are 60 minutes in 1 hour.
• Alberto practiced his flute for 7 hr.	• To change minutes to hours, divide by 60.

Draw Conclusions

360 min = 6 hr

2. Solve the problem. 360 ÷ 6 = 6 hours; 6 hr < 7 hr; Alberto practiced longer

3. Describe the strategy you used. Possible answer: I wrote a number sentence and compared the numbers of hours.

Examine the information, and use what you already know to draw conclusions. Solve.

4. On Friday, Pam's niece was just 18 months old. Peter's niece was exactly 64 weeks old. What is the age of Peter's niece in months? Whose niece is older?

   about 16 months; Pam's niece

5. Jack worked in the yard for 2 hours. His brother, Jake, worked in the yard for 180 minutes. How many hours did Jake work? Who worked in the yard longer?

   3 hr; Jake

© Harcourt

Find the Mean

Write the correct answer.

Understand ➤ Plan ➤ Solve ➤ Check

1. Jana went to a 3:30 P.M. movie. The movie lasted one and one-half hours. If the drive home took 45 minutes, at what time did Jana get home?

_____5:45 P.M._____

2. Jeffrey bought 3 pounds of apples at $1.29 per pound and paid with a $10.00 bill. How much change should he receive?

_____$6.13_____

3. The four 4th grade classes at Ritchie Elementary have 20, 18, 20, and 22 students. What is the mean class size?

_____20 students_____

4. Sara's basketball team scored 55, 60, 70, 47, 53, 49, 72, 61, 57, and 66 points during this season's games. Find the mean number of points scored.

_____59 points_____

Choose the letter of the correct answer.

5. What type of graph should the science teacher use to record the growth of a bean plant throughout February?

   A stem-and-leaf plot
   B bar graph
   C line graph
   D double-bar graph

6. Steve read a dozen books whose lengths were 95, 82, 92, 82, 89, 111, 98, 43, 76, 108, 67, and 89 pages. What was the average length of the books?

   F 98 pages   H 86 pages
   G 89 pages   J 82 pages

7. What is the range of pages in Steve's books?

   A 68
   B 82
   C 88
   D 92

8. Jenna worked four shifts as a waitress. Her tips were $22.10, $19.80, $12.90, and $25.60. What is the average tip amount?

   F $80.00   H $20.10
   G $21.00   J $20.00

9. **Write About It** Explain your solution to Problem 7.

Possible answer: To find the range, I subtracted the lowest number of

pages from the highest number of pages. 111 − 43 = 68, so the range is 68.

Name _____

Divisibility Rules

Write the correct answer.

1. Jolene's house number is 2735. Is 2,735 divisible by 2, 3, 5, 9, or 10?

_____5_____

2. Mel walks 12 blocks to school each day. He goes to school from Monday through Friday. How many blocks does he walk in one week to school?

_____60 blocks_____

3. Riley wants to buy a magazine that costs $4.50. He has $3.15. How much more money does he need to buy the magazine?

_____$1.35_____

4. Is 960 divisible by 2, 3, 5, 9, or 10?

_____2, 3, 5, and 10_____

Choose the letter of the correct answer.

5. Which number is **not** divisible by 3?

A 24
B 89
C 414
D 501

6. Which shows an example of the Distributive Property?

F $5 + 10 = 10 + 5$
G $(10 \times 5) \times 2 = 10 \times (5 \times 2)$
H $15 \times 2 = (10 \times 2) + (5 \times 2)$
J $15 \times 2 = 2 \times 15$

7. There are 45 horses on the farm. Each stable holds 9 horses. How many stables are on the farm?

A 5 stables   C 54 stables
B 36 stables   D 405 stables

8. Which number is divisible by 9?

F 1,209
G 3,258
H 5,045
J 9,002

9. **Write About It** Explain how you found your answer to Problem 8?

Possible answer: A number is divisible by 9 if the sum of its digits is divisible by 9. The sum of the digits of 3,258 is 18 and 18 is divisible by 9.

Factors and Multiples

Write the correct answer.

Understand ➡ Plan ➡ Solve ➡ Check

1. Solve.

$$7,942 \times 87$$

690,954

2. Solve.

$$9,000 \times 100$$

900,000

3. Write the first 6 multiples of 8.

8, 16, 24, 32, 40, 48

4. List the factors of 100.

1, 2, 4, 5, 10, 20, 25, 50, 100

Choose the letter of the correct answer.

5. The factors of 36 are:

A 0, 2, 4, 6, 9

B 1, 6, 36, 72

C 1, 3, 4, 8, 9

D 1, 2, 3, 4, 6, 9, 12, 18, 36

6. Which number completes the equation?

$$8 \times \underline{\ ?\ } = 72$$

F 7

G 8

H 9

J 16

7. Will has 24 guppies. He wants to share them with some friends. Which is **not** a way he could share the fish?

A 3 guppies to 6 friends

B 6 guppies to 4 friends

C 8 guppies to 3 friends

D 12 guppies to 2 friends

8. Sarah is sending cookies to her friends. She made 32 cookies, and she would like to put 8 in each package. What equation can you use to show the number of friends, m, to whom Sarah can send her cookies?

F $32 \times 8 = m$

G $8 \div m = 32$

H $32 \div 8 = m$

J $8 \div m = 1$

9. Write About It Explain how you used factors to solve Problem 7.

Possible answer: I thought of basic facts for the number 24.

The number of guppies each friend shared times the number of friends must equal 24.

Prime and Composite Numbers

Understand ➡ Plan ➡ Solve ➡ Check

Write the correct answer.

1. Sally has 7 friends. Each one wants to take home 3 pieces of carrot cake. If there are 6 slices in one carrot cake, how many cakes will Sally need?

_____ 4 cakes _____

2. Chuck bought colored notebooks. He spent $6.00 on red notebooks, $8.00 on green notebooks, and $12.00 on yellow notebooks. If each notebook cost $2.00, how many notebooks did he buy altogether?

_____ 13 notebooks _____

3. Is the number 80 prime or composite? Explain.

_____ composite; 80 is 40 × 2, so it _____

_____ must be composite. _____

4. In how many ways can you stack 27 books equally? Name them.

_____ 4 ways; 1 pile of 27 books, _____

_____ 3 piles of 9 books, 9 piles of _____

_____ 3 books, 27 piles of 1 book _____

Choose the letter of the correct answer.

5. Amy is 5 years younger than Josh. She is twice Sam's age. Josh's age is less than 16. Sam is older than 4. How old is Sam?

   A 4   **C** 7

   B 5   **D** 8

6. In which set are all the numbers prime?

   F 3, 12, 36   **H** 5, 31, 53

   G 18, 28, 48   **J** 7, 27, 57

7. In which set are all the numbers composite?

   A 4, 44, 144   **C** 56, 43, 39

   B 31, 35, 39   **D** 11, 21, 31

8. Which is **not** a way you could place 60 cans in equal rows?

   F 2 rows of 30   **H** 3 rows of 20

   G 6 rows of 10   **J** 4 rows of 13

9. **Write About It** Explain how you solved Problem 5.

_____ Possible answer: I used predict and test to try the given numbers 4, 5, 7, _____

_____ and 8 for Sam's age. _____

Form Mental Images

Understand ➡ Plan ➡ Solve ➡ Check

Sometimes it is helpful to **visualize**, or form a mental image of, the information in a problem. Using the details or facts to form mental images can help you organize and understand information. Read the following paragraph.

VOCABULARY
visualize

> Jeannie is painting a border along the ceiling of her room. She is painting elephants, giraffes, and snakes in a pattern. First she paints an elephant, then a giraffe, then two snakes. She repeats this pattern around the entire room. Which animal will be 7th in her painting?

1. Use the details to make a mental picture. Then use the words to describe what you see. Possible answers given.

Details	Visualize/Form Mental Images
Jeannie is painting a border.	Girl on a ladder painting
First she paints an elephant.	Elephant painted on the wall
Then she paints a giraffe.	Elephant and giraffe painted on wall
Then she paints two snakes.	Pattern: elephant, giraffe, two snakes
She repeats the pattern.	Pattern: elephant, giraffe, snake, snake

2. Solve the problem. Snake; Pattern: elephant, giraffe, snake, snake, ...

3. Describe the strategy you used. Possible answer: I visualized the pattern and counted through to the seventh animal, which was a snake.

Form mental images to solve.

4. The first row of Lara's garden has carrots. Then there are two rows of radishes and one row of lettuce. This pattern continues. What is in the 8th row of Lara's garden?

   lettuce

5. On Monday Haley worked at the concession stand for 25 minutes. Each day he worked 25 minutes more than the day before. How long did he work on Friday?

   125 minutes

© Harcourt

Square Numbers

Write the correct answer.

Understand ➡ Plan ➡ Solve ➡ Check

1. Leon uses 25 tiles to make a square mosaic. All of the tiles are the same size. How many tiles are on each side of the mosaic?

   _____5 tiles_____

2. Ms. Dixon buys granola bars to share with her class. There are 6 granola bars in each box. List the first 5 multiples of 6. How many granola bars are in 5 boxes?

   6, 12, 18, 24, 30; 30 granola bars

3. Diedre walks 3 miles on Monday and on Friday, 4 miles on Tuesday and on Thursday, and 1 mile on Wednesday. What is the mean number of miles she walks?

   _____3 miles_____

4. Name the square number and the square root for the array.

   _____16, 4_____

Choose the letter of the correct answer.

5. Which number is composite?

   A 2
   B 3
   C 9
   D 11

6. Which number is divisible by 3?

   F 701
   G 702
   H 712
   J 713

7. What is the square root of 9?

   A 3
   B 6
   C 18
   D 81

8. Each side of a square array has 6 square tiles. How many tiles are in the array in all?

   F 6 tiles
   G 12 tiles
   H 18 tiles
   J 36 tiles

9. **Write About It** How did you find your answer to Problem 1?

   Possible answer: I found the square root of 25 by asking myself what

   number times itself equals 25: 5.

Lines and Rays

Write the correct answer.

Understand ➡ Plan ➡ Solve ➡ Check

1. Mary Ann buys a sandwich for $2.25, a banana for $0.65, and milk for $0.90. How much does she spend altogether?

_____ $3.80 _____

2. Which figure does the surface of this sheet of paper most resemble: *point*, *line*, *line segment*, or *plane*?

_____ plane _____

3. Evaluate: (15 − 7) + (7 × 3).

_____ 29 _____

4. Which figure does the answer blank below most resemble: *point*, *line*, *line segment*, or *plane*?

_____ line segment _____

Choose the letter of the correct answer.

5. Tyler has 5 books of stamps. There are 25 stamps in each book. How many stamps does he have in all?

A 5 stamps

B 30 stamps

C 105 stamps

D 125 stamps

6. Which statement about lines is **not** true?

F They go on in both directions.

G They are straight paths of points.

H They can be curved.

J They have no endpoints

7. Which geometric figure best describes the hour hand on a clock?

A point   C line

B ray   D plane

8. Ned has five coins in his pocket. Which cannot be the total value of the coins?

F $1.05   H $0.25

G $0.29   J $0.20

9. **Write About It** Describe the strategy you used to solve Problem 7?

Possible answer: I drew a picture of a clock and noticed that the hour

hand looks like a ray.

Measure and Classify Angles

Understand → Plan → Solve → Check

Write the correct answer.

1. Measure the angle with a protractor.

55°
_____

2. Measure the angle with a protractor.

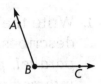

110°
_____

3. Carl has 10 quarters and 2 dimes. How much money does Carl have?

$2.70
_____

4. Sondra had $2.78 in the bank. Three weeks later she had 4 times this amount. How much money did she have then?

$11.12
_____

Choose the letter of the correct answer.

5. Carol needs 21 square feet of wallpaper and Sarah needs 53 square feet of wallpaper. How much wallpaper do they need in all?

   A 76 sq ft   C 74 sq ft
   B 75 sq ft   D 73 sq ft

6. Which best describes this angle?

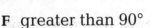

   F greater than 90°
   G less than 90°
   H 90°
   J 180°

7. Which best describes this angle?

   A obtuse
   B acute
   C right
   D straight

8. Heidi practices piano for 25 minutes. If she starts practicing at 3:55 P.M., what time should she stop?

   F 3:30 P.M.
   G 4:20 P.M.
   H 4:25 P.M.
   J 4:30 P.M.

9. **Write About It** How do you use a protractor to find the measure of the angle in Problem 2?

Possible answer: Line up the center mark and the 0°

mark on one of the rays. Then read the measurement of

the angle where the other ray passes through the scale.

Line Relationships

Write the correct answer.

1. Write the term that best describes the line relationship: *parallel, perpendicular,* or *intersecting.*

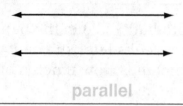

<u>   parallel   </u>

2. Write the term that best describes the line relationship: *parallel, perpendicular,* or *intersecting.*

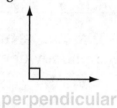

<u>   perpendicular   </u>

3. Write *rays, lines,* or *line segments,* to describe the figures in Problem 1.

<u>   lines   </u>

4. Write *acute, obtuse,* or *right* to describe the angle formed by the rays in Problem 2.

<u>   right   </u>

Choose the letter of the correct answer.

5. Which name describes the angle?

  A acute   **C** right
  B obtuse   **D** straight

6. Which term describes the figure?

  F plane   **H** point
  G line segment   **J** line

7. Emilio draws two parallel lines. Which statement about the lines is true?

  A They form two angles.
  B They form four acute angles.
  C They intersect.
  D They do not intersect.

8. Lisa gets a quarter, a dime, and 2 pennies change from a $20 bill. How much did she pay?

  F $20.67
  G $19.73
  H $19.63
  J $19.37

9. Write About It Describe the strategy you used to solve Problem 8.

Possible answer: I drew pictures of the coins, then I wrote

their value and subtracted that from $20.00.

Make Inferences

Understand ➡ Plan ➡ Solve ➡ Check

To **make inferences** means to draw conclusions based on the given information. In order to make an inference, you must examine all of the given information. Read the following problem.

VOCABULARY
make inferences

In the morning, Eric leaves his house and rides 4 blocks south, 6 blocks west, 5 blocks south, and 4 blocks east. In the afternoon, Eric rides from home to his cousin Fred's house. Eric rides the same route as in the morning, and then rides 4 more blocks going east. What inference can you make about where Eric's house is compared to Fred's?

1. Examine the information given in the problem. Then make inferences about that information.

Information	Inference
In the morning, Eric rides ___4___ blocks south and ___6___ blocks west. He rides ___5___ blocks south and ___4___ blocks east.	Possible answer: Eric is south of his home since he does not ride north at all. Eric is west of his home since he rides more blocks west than east.
In the afternoon, Eric rides ___4___ more blocks going east.	Possible answer: Eric is east of his home, since he rode more blocks total going east than going west.

2. Solve the problem. Eric's home is 9 blocks north and 2 blocks west of Fred's.

3. Describe the strategy you used. Possible answer: I drew a diagram.

Make inferences to solve.

4. Leslie has two ribbons. One ribbon is 5 inches long. The other ribbon is 3 times as long. Amanda's ribbon is longer than both of Leslie's ribbons placed end to end. What inferences can you make about Amanda's ribbon?

   Possible answer: The ribbon must be longer than 20 inches.

5. From work, Mr. Kent drives 52 miles east, 36 miles north, and then another 28 miles east to his home. His coworker, Mrs. Young, has a shorter ride home than Mr. Kent. What inference can you make about the location of Mrs. Young's home from work?

   Possible answer: Mrs. Young's home is less than 116 miles from work.

Name _____

Polygons

Write the correct answer.

Understand ➡ Plan ➡ Solve ➡ Check

1. Name the polygon and tell if it is *regular* or *not regular*.

___regular pentagon___

2. Randy has 35 model cars. He keeps them in 5 boxes. Each box holds the same number of model cars. How many model cars are in each box?

___7 model cars___

3. Draw a triangle that is **not** regular.

___Check students' drawings.___

4. Multiply.
   23
   × 17

   ___391___

Choose the letter of the correct answer.

5. A sign has 6 sides. Two sides are the same length. The other sides are different lengths. Which polygon best describes the sign?

   A regular hexagon
   B regular octagon
   C hexagon
   D octagon

6. Which number is a prime number?

   F 15
   G 21
   H 29
   J 33

7. Which best describes the polygon?

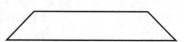

   A triangle
   B quadrilateral
   C pentagon
   D hexagon

8. Claire buys a sandwich for $2.75. She pays with a $5 bill. What is her change?

   F $2.25
   G $2.75
   H $3.25
   J $3.75

9. **Write About It** How did you choose your answer to Problem 5?

   ___Possible answer: I counted the number of sides; a figure with 6 sides___

   ___is a hexagon; the sides are different lengths so the figure is not regular.___

Name _____

Classify Triangles

Write the correct answer.

Understand ▶ Plan ▶ Solve ▶ Check

1. Matt has a sign in the shape of a triangle. The sign has 2 sides that are equal. Classify the shape of Matt's sign as *isosceles*, *scalene*, or *equilateral*.

    isosceles

2. Jessica's book has 128 pages. She reads 20 pages each day for 3 days. How many pages does Jessica have left to read?

    68 pages

3. How many equal sides does a scalene triangle have?

4. Write twelve thousand, three hundred ninety-four in expanded form.

    $10,000 + 2,000 + 300 + 90 + 4$

Choose the letter of the correct answer.

5. A pack of gum costs $0.53. If Patrick buys 9 packs of gum, how much money will he need?

    A $4.75   C $4.77
    B $4.76   D $4.78

6. Find the value: $12 (3 + 1)$.

    F 15   H 37
    G 36   J 48

7. Draw an isosceles triangle. How many equal sides must an isosceles triangle have?

    A 0
    B 2
    C 3
    D 4

8. Classify the triangle by the lengths of its sides and by the measure of its angles.

    F scalene, acute
    G scalene, right
    H isosceles, acute
    J isosceles, obtuse

9. **Write About It** How did you choose your answer to Problem 8?

    Possible answer: I know that the lengths of the sides are all different so it is scalene; there is one right angle so it is a right triangle.

Name _____

Classify Quadrilaterals

Understand ➡ Plan ➡ Solve ➡ Check

Write the correct answer.

1. This quadrilateral has only 1 pair of parallel sides. It has no right angles. What quadrilateral is it?

_____trapezoid_____

2. Name the quadrilateral shown below.

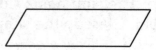

_____parallelogram_____

3. Harold notices that the sign, "Road Slippery When Wet," has 5 angles. What kind of polygon is the sign?

_____pentagon_____

4. Which quadrilateral is most like the doorway you use to enter your classroom?

_____rectangle or parallelogram_____

Choose the letter of the correct answer.

5. Which of the kinds of lines and angles are *not* in the figure below?

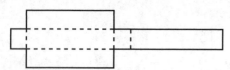

   A parallel lines
   B right angles
   C perpendicular lines
   D acute angles

6. Bart walks 12 dogs that belong to his neighbors to make extra money. He takes 2 walks each day with each dog. How many walks does he take in a week?

   F 124 walks
   G 148 walks
   H 168 walks
   J 180 walks

7. Which of the following letters does *not* contain parallel lines?

   A E
   B N
   C A
   D H

8. Which of the following is a good estimate for the product?

$$13 \times 289$$

   F 300
   G 2,000
   H 3,000
   J 30,000

9. **Write About It** Explain why this statement is true: All squares are rectangles but not all rectangles are squares.

   Possible answer: Both a rectangle and a square are parallelograms

   with 4 right angles, but a square must have 4 equal sides.

© Harcourt

Use Graphic Aids

Understand ➡ Plan ➡ Solve ➡ Check

Using **graphic aids** such as a graph, table, or diagram can help you see relationships in a problem. Read the following problem.

VOCABULARY
graphic aids

Six groups are going on a tour. The table at the right gives the group names and the number of people in each group. The tour guide needs to divide each group into smaller groups of either 3 or 5. The tour guide made this Venn diagram:

Tour Groups						
Group Name	A	B	C	D	E	F
Number	24	25	33	20	27	35

Groups that can be divided into groups of 3

Groups that can be divided into groups of 5

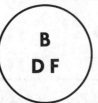

1. Answer each question about the Venn diagram.

   a. What does each label tell you?

   Possible answer: What kinds of groups have

   been placed into each circle.

   b. Are there any groups that belong in both circles? Explain.

   Possible answer: No; None of these groups can be divided

   into groups of both 3 and 5.

Use a Venn diagram to help you solve each problem.   Check students' diagrams.

2. Sort these numbers into those that are *Divisible by 4* and *Not Divisible by 4*.

   2, 3, 4, 6, 8, 10, 12

3. Sort these numbers into those that are *Divisible by 2* and *Divisible by 3*.

   2, 3, 4, 8, 9, 10, 14, 15, 20, 21, 22, 26, 27, 28

© Harcourt

Circles

Write the correct answer.

Understand ➡ Plan ➡ Solve ➡ Check

1. The diameter of one circle is 2 feet longer than the diameter of another circle. Together the diameters equal 20 feet. How long is each diameter?

_____9 ft and 11 ft_____

2. If Andy can run 6 miles in an hour, how many miles can he run in 10 minutes?

_____1 mi_____

3. If the radius of a circle is 38 centimeters, what is the length of its diameter?

_____76 cm_____

4. Suu Kim has 30 math problems to do for homework. If it takes Suu 1 hour to do 15 problems, how long will it take her to do all of her math homework?

_____2 hours_____

Choose the letter of the correct answer.

5. Round 142,456 to the nearest hundred.

   A 142,000
   B 142,400
   C 142,460
   D 142,500

6. What is the radius of a circle with a diameter of 92 inches?

   F 45 inches
   G 46 inches
   H 184 inches
   J 186 inches

7. Which best describes $\overline{AB}$ in the picture below?

   A radius
   B ray
   C diameter
   D chord

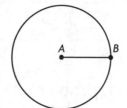

8. What is the diameter of a basketball rim if the radius is 9 inches?

   F 18 inches
   G 19 inches
   H 23 inches
   J 27 inches

9. **Write About It** Explain how you found the diameter in Problem 3?

   Possible answer: I multiplied the radius by 2.

_____

Turns and Symmetry

Write the correct answer.

1. Does the figure have rotational symmetry? Write *yes* or *no*.

_____yes_____

2. Does the figure have rotational symmetry? Write *yes* or *no*.

_____no_____

3. Tell whether the hour hand of a clock that begins at 12 has been turned 90°, 180°, 270°, or 360° when it is 3:00.

_____90°_____

4. I am a 3-digit odd number. My tens digit is one less than my hundreds digit but two more than my ones digit. The sum of my digits is 20. Who am I?

_____875_____

Choose the letter of the correct answer.

5. Jimmy makes a $\frac{3}{4}$ turn in his car. Which of the following tells how many degrees he turned?

A 90°   **C** 270°
B 180°   **D** 360°

6. 5,422
   $\times\ 67$

F 324,657   **H** 363,274
G 353,128   **J** 373,274

7. An airplane flew 8 hours to New York, 9 hours to Los Angeles, and then 4 hours to Cincinnati. How many hours did the airplane fly?

A 288 hours   **C** 21 hours
B 22 hours   **D** 20 hours

8. $\overleftrightarrow{AB}$ and $\overleftrightarrow{CD}$ are parallel. Which of the following is also true?

F They are intersecting.
G They are perpendicular.
H They do not meet.
J They form an angle.

9. Write About It Describe the method you used to test for rotational symmetry in Problems 1 and 2.

Possible answer: I traced the figure, held down the tracing with a

pencil point at the center, and turned it to see if it lined up with the

original figure.

Congruent and Similar Figures

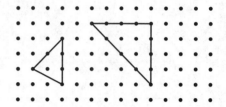

Write the correct answer.

1. Tell whether the two figures appear to be *congruent*, *similar*, *both*, or *neither*.

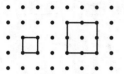

_____ similar _____

2. Do the two figures appear to be *congruent*, *similar*, *both*, or *neither*?

_____ neither _____

3. What are all the prime numbers between 12 and 18?

_____ 13; 17 _____

4. Kim has $25.78. Juan has twice as much money as Kim who has twice as much as Mark. How much money do they have in all?

_____ $90.23 _____

Choose the letter of the correct answer

5. What kind of lines always form four right angles?

A parallel   **C** intersecting
B congruent   **D** perpendicular

6. What kind of angle does the corner of a rectangle form?

F right   **H** acute
G obtuse   **J** parallel

7. The word *kilobyte* means "one thousand bytes" of information. A kilobyte is actually 1,024 bytes of information. How many more than 1,000 bytes are actually in a kilobyte of information?

A 2 bytes   **C** 24 bytes
B 16 bytes   **D** 1,000 bytes

8. Which of the following does *not* have to be true about two congruent figures?

F They have the same size.
G They have the same shape.
H They have the same number of sides.
J They are in the same position.

9. Write about It Explain why you chose the answer you did in Problem 7.

Possible answer: I subtracted 1,000 kilobytes from 1,024, the actual

kilobytes, to get 24 more kilobytes.

Name _____

Paraphrase Information

Understand ➡ **Plan** ➡ **Solve** ➡ **Check**

Sometimes it is helpful to **paraphrase,** or state again in your own words, what a problem is asking you to do.

VOCABULARY
paraphrase

Read the following problem.

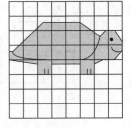

> Suppose you want to make a larger copy of the picture of the turtle at the right. How could you make a copy of the figure, square by square, and make a larger picture?

1. Complete the sentence to paraphrase what the problem is asking you to do. Possible answer given.

   The problem asks me to

   make a larger picture of the turtle, with exactly
   _____

   the same shape.
   _____

2. Solve the problem. Check students' drawings. They should draw the same turtle on larger grid paper.

3. Describe the strategy you used.

   Possible answer: I copied it square by square
   _____

   onto grid paper with larger squares.
   _____

   _____

Paraphrase what each problem is asking you to do. Solve.

4. Suppose you want to make a smaller picture of the kite at the right. Use 1-cm grid paper. Then copy the figure, square by square, to make a smaller picture. Check students' drawings. They

   should show the same kite on 1-cm grid paper.

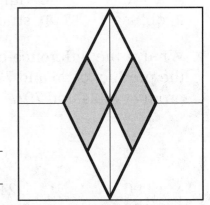

5. Suppose you want to make a larger picture of the design at the right. Use 1-inch grid paper. Then copy the figure, square by square, to make a larger picture. Check students' drawings. They

   should show the same emblem on 1-in. grid paper.

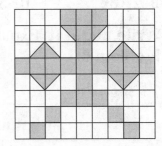

© Harcourt

Reading Strategy **PS99**

Name _____

Transformations

Write the correct answer.

1. Do the two figures appear to be *congruent*, *similar*, *both*, or *neither*?

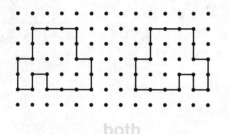

both
_____

2. Draw a reflection of the figure shown below.

Check students' drawings.
_____

3. Write *translation*, *reflection*, or *rotation* to describe how the figures in Problem 1 were moved.

reflection
_____

4. Mr. Bond drives 34 miles east, 28 miles south, and then another 17 miles east. How any miles does Mr. Bond drive in all?

79 miles
_____

Choose the letter of the correct answer

5. What kind of angle is the corner of this page?

A acute   **C** right
B obtuse   D straight

6. Which of these letters does *not* have a line of symmetry?

F A   **H** P
G D   J W

7. What is the difference between the product of 56 and 72 and the product of 24 and 79?

A 1,896   C 2,246
B 2,136   D 3,146

8. Which transformation describes how the figure on the left was moved?

F translation   H rotation
G reflection   J turn

9. Write about It Explain how you chose your answer to Problem 8.

Possible answer: I traced the figure and then was able to slide the figure

into the second figure. A slide is a translation.

Tessellations

Write the correct answer.

1. Does the figure tessellate? Write *yes* or *no*.

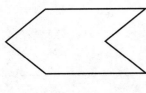

yes

2. Ellen has two ribbons. One ribbon is 8 inches long. The other ribbon is 4 times as long. How long are the ribbons when they are placed end to end?

40 in.

3. Does the figure tessellate? Write *yes* or *no*.

yes

4. Which type of angle does the answer blank below most resemble: *acute, right, obtuse,* or *straight*?

straight

Choose the letter of the correct answer

5. Which shape will *not* tessellate?

A square   **C** right triangle
B rectangle   **D** circle

6. Which geometric term best describes the tip of a pin?

F point   **H** line
G ray   **J** plane

7. Simplify: $3 \times (12 + 12)$.

A 48
B 72
C 147
D 432

8. Which number below is a composite number?

F 2
G 3
H 5
J 6

9. Write about It Explain how you found your answer to Problem 1.

Possible answer: I traced the figure and then checked to see if I could

cover the page without any gaps using the figure.

Geometric Patterns

Write the correct answer.

1. Draw the next figure in the pattern.

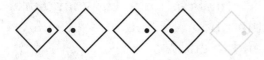

Check students' drawings.

2. A number is 8 more than twice 15. What is the number?

_____ 38 _____

3. Does the figure have rotational symmetry? Write *yes* or *no*.

_____ yes _____

4. Write a rule for the pattern.

Possible answer: Increase the number of sides by 1.

Choose the letter of the correct answer.

5. Tess walks 8 units north. Then she walks 6 units east, 2 units south, and 9 units west. How many units does Tess walk altogether?

   A 16 units   C 23 units
   B 22 units   D 25 units

6. Which statement is **not** true about rays?

   F They have one endpoint.
   G They are part of a line.
   H They continue without end in one direction.
   J They name an exact location in space.

7. How many degrees has the hour hand of a clock been turned from 12:00 when it is 3:00?

   A 90°
   B 180°
   C 270°
   D 360°

8. How many dots will be in the next figure in the pattern?

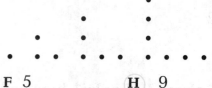

   F 5   H 9
   G 8   J 10

9. **Write About It** Explain how you found your answer to Problem 4.

Possible answer: I compared the figures to see how they were changing.

Name _____

Temperature: Fahrenheit

Understand ➡ Plan ➡ Solve ➡ Check

Write the correct answer.

1. Find the change in temperature from ⁻2°F to ⁺32°F.

   _____34°F_____

2. Multiply 27 × 318.

   _____8,586_____

3. Tina read 38 pages on Monday, 56 pages on Tuesday, and 41 pages on Wednesday. What was the mean number of pages she read each day?

   _____45 pages_____

4. Write 491,637 in expanded form.

   400,000 + 90,000 + 1,000 + 600 + 30 + 7

Choose the letter of the correct answer.

5. $9,070 − $4,388
   - **A** $4,682
   - **B** $5,318
   - **C** $5,392
   - **D** $13,458

6. Divide. 392 ÷ 4.
   - **F** 93
   - **G** 98
   - **H** 388
   - **J** 1,568

7. The temperature dropped 15 degrees after noon to 31°F. What was the temperature before it dropped?
   - **A** ⁻31°F
   - **B** ⁻15°F
   - **C** 16°F
   - **D** 46°F

8. The temperature was 55°F at 6 P.M., but it got colder as it got later. By 11 P.M., it was 32°F. How much did the temperature change?
   - **F** 32°F
   - **G** 23°F
   - **H** 12°F
   - **J** ⁻10°F

9. **Write About It** Explain how you solved Problem 1.

   Possible answer: I looked at a thermometer. A change from ⁻2 to 0 is 2 degrees, and a change from 0 to 32 is 32 degrees. The total change was 34 degrees Fahrenheit.

Temperature: Celsius
Write the correct answer.

1. The thermometer shows the water temperature in °C. The air temperature is 30°C. What is the difference in temperature?

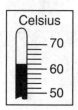

32°C

2. The thermometer shows the noon temperature in °C. The midnight temperature was 6°C. How many degrees did the temperature rise between midnight and noon?

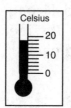

12°C

3. The average January temperature in San Juan, Puerto Rico, is 24°C. The average January temperature in Oslo, Norway, is ⁻4°C. What is the difference in the average January temperature of these two cities?

28°C

4. The temperature of a bowl of soup is 85°C. If the soup cools down 12°C, what will its temperature be after cooling?

73°C

Choose the letter of the correct answer.

5. Find the change in temperature from 10°F to ⁻20°F.

   A 10°F C 30°F
   B 20°F D 40°F

6. Find the elapsed time between half past noon and a quarter to one.

   F 15 min H 45 min
   G 30 min J 1 hr 15 min

7. Which is the most reasonable estimate for the temperature inside your freezer?

   A 30°C
   B 10°C
   C ⁻10°C
   D ⁻100°C

8. Chad, Linda, Janey, and Josh are in line. Linda is right behind Josh. The boys are between the girls. In what order are they?

   F Josh, Linda, Chad, Janey
   G Chad, Josh, Linda, Janey
   H Janey, Josh, Linda, Chad
   J Janey, Chad, Josh, Linda

9. **Write About It** Describe the method you used to solve Problem 8.

   Possible answer: I wrote the names on 4 pieces of paper and moved
   _____
   them around to find the answer.

Explore Negative Numbers

Understand ➡ Plan ➡ Solve ➡ Check

Write the correct answer.

1. The record high and low temperatures in Boise, Idaho, are 111°F (July 1960) and ⁻25°F (December 1990). What is the difference between these temperatures?

_____136°F_____

2. Compare. Write < or > for the ●.

⁻6 ● ⁺5

_____<_____

3. Gertie and Pete want to build a wooden fence around the backyard for the new puppy. The cost of the fencing is $10.50 per foot, and they need 9 yards. How much will the fencing cost them?

_____$283.50_____

4. Jim ran the length of his driveway (10 yards), walked the length of the neighbor's sidewalk (40 feet), ran the length of the track (200 feet), and ran home (50 feet). How many total feet did he run?

_____280 feet_____

Choose the letter of the correct answer.

5. The temperature at the top of the mountain was 30 degrees colder than at the base of the mountain, where the thermometer read 5°C. What was the temperature at the top of the mountain?

A ⁻35°C   C ⁺25°C
B ⁻25°C   D ⁺30°C

6. The Celsius temperatures were ⁻5°C, ⁺5°C, ⁻1°C, 0°C, ⁻2°C, ⁻3°C, and ⁺2°C during the week. What was the coldest temperature?

F ⁻5°C   H 0°C
G ⁻2°C   J ⁺5°C

7. Estimate.   3,465 + 8,787

A 12,000   C 10,000
B 11,000   D 9,000

8. Which is **not** true?

F 2 > ⁻7   H 4 > ⁻9
G ⁻3 > 9   J 2 > ⁻5

9. **Write About It** Explain your solution to Problem 5.

Possible answer: I drew a picture of a thermometer and counted

down 30 degrees from ⁺5. This gave me a temperature of ⁻25°C.

Multiple-Meaning Words

Understand ➡ Plan ➡ Solve ➡ Check

Some problems contain words that have more than one meaning. You can use information given in the problem to determine which meaning of the word is being used. Read the following problem.

> Mr. Wilson is an architect. He has a *degree* in architecture. He is designing an office building whose two wings sit at forty-five *degree* angles. As soon as the ground temperature is about 40 *degrees* Fahrenheit, construction crews can start working on the office building. The ground temperature is currently 28 degrees Fahrenheit. How much does the ground temperature have to rise before construction can begin?

1. Read the problem carefully to determine which word is used with more than one meaning. Write the word and the words around it. Write the meaning of the word each way it is being used. Possible answers are given.

Multiple-Meaning Word	Surrounding Words	Definition
degree	He has a degree in architecture.	a diploma earned in a particular subject
degree	two wings sit at forty-five degree angles	a unit of measuring angles
degree	the ground temperature is about 40 degrees	a unit of measuring temperature

2. Solve the problem. _____ 12°F _____

3. Describe the strategy you used. _____ Possible answer: I used the problem

solving strategy *write a number sentence.*

Read the problem carefully to determine which word or words might have multiple meanings. Underline the words. Solve.

4. The construction crew will pound nails to build the wooden frame for the office building. They ordered 200 pounds of nails. Each pound of nails has about 150 nails. About how many nails did they order in all?

_____ about 30,000 nails

5. The electric meter for the office building will be placed on the side of the building, 200 centimeters off the ground. How many meters high is this?

_____ 2 m

Explore Inequalities

 Understand ➡ Plan ➡ Solve ➡ Check

Write the correct answer.

1. Use the number line to graph three whole numbers that make this inequality true.

Check students' work.

$$\underline{\hspace{1cm}} + 2 \leq 10$$

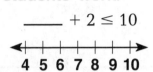

4 5 6 7 8 9 10

2. Tina is twice as old as Trevor. Together their ages add up to 18. How old is Trevor?

_____ 6 yr old

3. The temperature was 42°F at 8 A.M. By 11 A.M., the temperature was 54°F. How much did the temperature change?

_____ 12°F

4. Which of the numbers 12, 13, and 14 make this inequality true?

$$\underline{\hspace{1cm}} > 12$$

_____ 13, 14

Choose the letter of the correct answer.

5. Which of the following numbers makes this inequality true?

$$\underline{\hspace{1cm}} - 3 < 2$$

A 10   **C** 5

B 6   **D** 3

6. Find the median.

26, 32, 24, 21, 32

F 24   **H** 27

G 26   **J** 32

7. A florist needs the stems of her flowers to be at least 8 inches long. Which of the following stems is not long enough?

A 7 in.   **C** 10 in.

B 8 in.   **D** 12 in.

8. Which of these numbers is prime?

F 27   **H** 49

G 31   **J** 55

9. Write About It How did you choose your answer to Problem 5?

Possible answer: I put each of the numbers into the inequality until I found the one that made a true number sentence.

Use a Coordinate Grid

Write the correct answer.

Understand → Plan → Solve → Check

1. Write the ordered pair for each point on the coordinate grid.

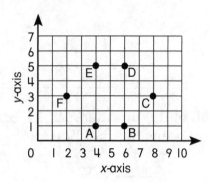

A, (4,1); B, (6,1); C, (8,3);

D, (6,5); E, (4,5); F, (2,3)

2. Which axis on a coordinate grid is a vertical line?

_____ y-axis _____

3. The product of two numbers is 96. Their difference is 10. What are the numbers?

_____ 6 and 16 _____

Choose the letter of the correct answer.

4. In an ordered pair, what is the first number called?

   A x-axis

   B y-axis

   C x-coordinate

   D y-coordinate

5. To locate a point at (2,3) where do you start?

   F at 3

   G at 2

   H at 1

   J at 0

6. How much greater than 949,146 is 1,010,103?

   A 171,249

   B 70,967

   C 60,957

   D 59,057

7. Roger has 3 quarters, 2 dimes, and 5 pennies. How much money does he have in all?

   F $0.95

   G $1.00

   H $1.10

   J $1.25

8. Write About It What can you conclude about a point that has 0 as one of its coordinates?

Possible answer: It lies along one of the axes of the coordinate grid.

© Harcourt

Read and Write Fractions

Write the correct answer.

1. Write a fraction for the shaded part.

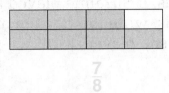

$\frac{7}{8}$

2. Shade the model to show the fraction $\frac{4}{5}$.

Check that $\frac{4}{5}$ is shaded.

3. Tia's family is having a reunion. 117 people will be seated, 8 to a table. How many tables will be needed?

15 tables

4. Harry is setting traps for lobsters. Each trap can hold about 30 lobsters. If he sets 82 traps, about how many lobsters could he catch?

about 2,400 lobsters

Choose the letter of the correct answer.

5. Which type of graph is best for showing the change in data over time?

   A bar graph   **C** stem-and-leaf plot

   B double-bar graph   **D** line graph

6. Which fraction shows the part of the model that is *not* shaded?

   F $\frac{1}{5}$ **H** $\frac{3}{5}$

   G $\frac{2}{5}$ **J** $\frac{2}{3}$

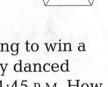

7. A building has 7 floors. A book company takes up 3 floors. An ad agency takes up 2 floors. A design firm takes up the remaining floors. What fraction of the building is used by the design firm?

   A $\frac{1}{7}$ **C** $\frac{3}{7}$

   B $\frac{2}{7}$ **D** $\frac{4}{7}$

8. Rosa and Tim are trying to win a dance marathon. They danced from 6:50 A.M. until 11:45 P.M. How long did they dance?

   F 5 hr   **H** 17 hr 5 min

   G 17 hr   **J** 16 hr 55 min

9. **Write About It** Explain how you chose the fraction to write for Problem 1.

Possible answer: I counted all of the equal parts in the figure and used

8 as the denominator; I counted the shaded parts and used 7 as the

numerator.

Name _____

Equivalent Fractions

Understand ➡ Plan ➡ Solve ➡ Check

Write the correct answer.

1. Find two fractions equivalent to $\frac{1}{2}$.

Possible answer: $\frac{2}{4}, \frac{3}{6}$

2. A hockey game is divided into 3 periods. If Suzanne played for 2 periods, write the fraction of the game she played.

$\frac{2}{3}$

3. Write 30 as a product of prime factors.

$2 \times 3 \times 5$

4. Find a fraction that is equivalent to $\frac{3}{4}$ and has a denominator of 8.

$\frac{6}{8}$

Choose the letter of the correct answer.

5. Which fraction is *not* equivalent to $\frac{3}{12}$?

A $\frac{1}{2}$

B $\frac{1}{4}$

C $\frac{2}{8}$

D $\frac{6}{24}$

6. Which of these numbers is prime?

F 30

G 47

H 99

J 100

7. Which fraction is equivalent to $\frac{9}{10}$?

A $\frac{3}{4}$

B $\frac{18}{20}$

C $\frac{8}{10}$

D $1\frac{1}{9}$

8. Talia jogged 46 times last year. About how many times did she jog each month?

F 5 times

G 4 times

H 3 times

J 2 times

9. Write About It Explain how you answered Problem 5.

Possible answer: I changed the fractions to simplest form and saw some

were equal to $\frac{1}{4}$. Only $\frac{1}{2}$ was not equivalent.

Compare and Order Fractions

Understand → Plan → Solve → Check

Write the correct answer.

1. Write a number sentence using
   $<$, $>$, or $=$ that compares the two
   fractions shown in the models.

   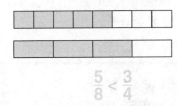

   $\frac{5}{8} < \frac{3}{4}$

2. Write a fraction to show the part of
   the group that is shaded.

   $\frac{3}{10}$

3. On the soccer team, $\frac{5}{9}$ of the
   players are girls. On the field
   hockey team, $\frac{5}{6}$ of the players are
   girls. Which team has a greater
   fraction of girls?

   the field hockey team

4. Leonard stood on the corner and
   counted the cars that went by. Out
   of 22 cars, 17 were taxis. What
   fraction of the cars were taxis?

   $\frac{17}{22}$ of the cars

Choose the letter of the correct answer.

5. Which set of fractions is ordered
   from *least* to *greatest*?

   A $\frac{2}{3}, \frac{2}{7}, \frac{2}{5}$ C $\frac{1}{5}, \frac{1}{9}, \frac{1}{7}$

   B $\frac{3}{8}, \frac{3}{7}, \frac{3}{4}$ D $\frac{4}{5}, \frac{4}{7}, \frac{4}{9}$

6. Which set of fractions is ordered
   from *greatest* to *least*?

   F $\frac{3}{8}, \frac{5}{8}, \frac{7}{8}$ H $\frac{1}{5}, \frac{3}{5}, \frac{4}{5}$

   G $\frac{2}{9}, \frac{7}{9}, \frac{5}{9}$ J $\frac{6}{7}, \frac{5}{7}, \frac{2}{7}$

7. In Rowayton one spring, it rained
   on March 22 and every day after
   that until May 2. How many days
   in a row did it rain in Rowayton
   that spring?

   A 42 days
   B 39 days
   C 24 days
   D 12 days

8. In Mr. Wile's class, $\frac{3}{5}$ of the
   students try out for a play. In Ms.
   Kane's class, $\frac{6}{10}$ of the students try
   out. In which class does a greater
   fraction of the students try out?

   F Mr. Wile's
   G Ms. Kane's
   H Neither; the fractions are
     equivalent.
   J Not Here

9. **Write About It** What rule did you use to help you order the
   fractions in Problem 5?

   Possible answer: If two fractions have the same numerator, the fraction
   with the smaller denominator is the greater fraction.

Compare and Contrast

Understand ➤ Plan ➤ Solve ➤ Check

To solve some problems, you can compare and contrast information in a problem. Find things about the problem that are alike, and things that are different. Read the following problem.

A recipe calls for $\frac{3}{8}$ teaspoon of nutmeg, $\frac{1}{4}$ teaspoon of baking soda, and $\frac{2}{3}$ teaspoon of cinnamon. List the ingredients in order from the greatest amount to the least amount.

1. Write at least one way in which the fractions are alike in the **Compare** column. Write one way in which the fractions are different from each other in the **Contrast** column.
Possible answers are given.

Compare	Contrast
$\frac{3}{8}, \frac{1}{4},$ and $\frac{2}{3}$ are all less than 1. They are all parts of one whole.	$\frac{3}{8}, \frac{1}{4},$ and $\frac{2}{3}$ each have different denominators, so you cannot order them by comparing their numerators.

2. Solve the problem. $\frac{2}{3} > \frac{3}{8} > \frac{1}{4}$; cinnamon, nutmeg, baking soda

3. Describe the strategy you used. Possible answer: I made a model with fraction bars to order the fractions.

Compare and contrast the fractions in each problem. Solve.

4. Lizzie has $\frac{5}{8}$ gallon of red paint, $\frac{1}{8}$ gallon of blue paint, and $\frac{3}{8}$ gallon of white paint. List the paint colors in order from *least* to *greatest* amount.

blue, white, red

5. Scott has $\frac{3}{8}$ cup of nuts, $\frac{3}{4}$ cup of flour, and $\frac{2}{3}$ cup of sugar for baking cookies. List the ingredients in order from *greatest* to *least* amount.

flour, sugar, nuts

6. Al made punch for a party. The recipe called for $\frac{1}{2}$ gallon of orange juice, $\frac{3}{4}$ gallon of pineapple juice, and $\frac{4}{5}$ gallon of grape juice. List the ingredients in order from *greatest* to *least* amount.

grape juice, pineapple juice, orange juice

7. Karen used a recipe calling for $\frac{3}{4}$ cup of cherries, $\frac{5}{8}$ cup of water, and $\frac{1}{2}$ cup of honey. List the ingredients in order from *least* to *greatest* amount.

honey, water, cherries

© Harcourt

Mixed Numbers

Understand ➡ Plan ➡ Solve ➡ Check

Write the correct answer.

1. Write a mixed number for the number of figures that are shaded.

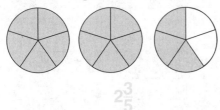

$2\frac{3}{5}$

_____

2. Write a mixed number for the number of figures that are shaded.

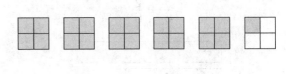

$5\frac{1}{4}$

3. A cake calls for 6 cups of flour. Elena uses whole wheat flour for $\frac{1}{2}$ of the recipe, white cake flour for $\frac{1}{3}$ of the recipe, and regular white flour for the remaining $\frac{1}{6}$ of the recipe. Which kind of flour does Elena use most in the cake?

whole wheat flour

_____

4. A bridge is divided into 9 equal sections. At one end of the bridge, 2 sections are over land. At the other end, 3 sections are over land. The rest are over water. What fraction of the bridge is over water?

$\frac{4}{9}$ of the bridge

_____

Choose the letter of the correct answer.

5. Which mixed number is equivalent to $\frac{9}{2}$?

A 18   **C** $9\frac{1}{4}$

B $9\frac{1}{2}$ **D** $4\frac{1}{2}$

6. Which mixed number is equivalent to $\frac{7}{3}$?

F $7\frac{1}{3}$ **H** $3\frac{1}{7}$

G $6\frac{1}{3}$ **J** $2\frac{1}{3}$

7. Amy plays a 30-minute cassette. The counter on her tape player moves from 0 to 360 while the tape is playing. Amy wants to play the last 10 minutes of the tape again. About how far back on the counter should she rewind the tape?

A to 300   **C** to 180

B to 240   **D** to 10

8. Renee bought $\frac{1}{2}$ pound of turkey, $\frac{3}{4}$ pound of cheese, and $\frac{1}{3}$ pound of tomatoes to make sandwiches. List the fractions in order from *least* to *greatest*.

F $\frac{1}{3}, \frac{1}{2}, \frac{3}{4}$ **H** $\frac{1}{2}, \frac{3}{4}, \frac{1}{3}$

G $\frac{3}{4}, \frac{1}{3}, \frac{1}{2}$ **J** $\frac{1}{3}, \frac{3}{4}, \frac{1}{2}$

9. Write About It Explain how you solved Problem 7.

Possible answer: Each minute moved the counter about 12. To go back

10 minutes, Amy should go back 10 × 12, or 120; 360 − 120 = 240.

Problem Solving PS113

Name _____

Add Like Fractions

Understand → Plan → Solve → Check

Write the correct answer.

1. Use the fraction bars to help you find the sum.

$$\frac{3}{6} + \frac{2}{6}$$

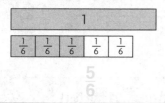

$$\frac{5}{6}$$

2. Use the fraction bars to help you find the sum.

$$\frac{1}{8} + \frac{3}{8}$$

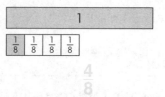

$$\frac{4}{8}$$

3. Steven measures the thickness of a board. He records the measurement as $\frac{5}{2}$ inches. Write his measurement using a mixed number.

$$2\frac{1}{2} \text{ in.}$$

4. In the fourth-grade class, $\frac{5}{8}$ of the students buy milk at lunch. In the fifth-grade class, $\frac{3}{4}$ of the students buy milk at lunch. In which class does a greater fraction of the class buy milk?

fifth grade

Choose the letter of the correct answer.

5. Find the sum. $\frac{4}{7} + \frac{2}{7}$

   A $\frac{2}{7}$ C $\frac{3}{4}$

   B $\frac{6}{14}$ D $\frac{6}{7}$

6. Which fraction is equivalent to $\frac{9}{18}$?

   F $\frac{2}{3}$ H $\frac{1}{2}$

   G $\frac{6}{9}$ J $\frac{27}{56}$

7. What are the missing numbers in the pattern?

   316, 332, 348, 364, ■, ■, 412

   A 378, 396   C 380, 386

   B 374, 390   D 380, 396

8. When Annette makes pumpkin pie, she adds $\frac{1}{4}$ teaspoon nutmeg, $\frac{1}{4}$ teaspoon cloves, and $\frac{1}{4}$ teaspoon allspice. What is the total amount of these three ingredients?

   F $\frac{3}{4}$ teaspoon   H $\frac{3}{8}$ teaspoon

   G $\frac{1}{2}$ teaspoon   J $\frac{1}{4}$ teaspoon

9. **Write About It** Write a rule for the pattern you saw in Problem 7.

   Possible answer: Add 16 to find the next number in the pattern.

   _____

   _____

Subtract Like Fractions

Write the correct answer.

1. Use fraction bars to find the difference.

$$\frac{8}{10} - \frac{3}{10}$$

$$\frac{5}{10}, \text{ or } \frac{1}{2}$$

2. Use fraction bars to find the difference.

$$\frac{8}{9} - \frac{4}{9}$$

$$\frac{4}{9}$$

3. Betty puts two strips of wood around the edge of a table. The cherry strip is $\frac{3}{4}$ inch wide, and the maple strip is $\frac{3}{8}$ inch wide. Which strip is wider?

the cherry strip

4. Claudia's pie recipe includes $\frac{1}{8}$ teaspoon nutmeg, $\frac{1}{4}$ teaspoon cloves, and $\frac{1}{2}$ teaspoon ginger. Order the three ingredients from *greatest* to *least* amount.

ginger, cloves, nutmeg

Choose the letter of the correct answer.

5. $\frac{8}{9} - \frac{2}{9} = \frac{?}{}$

A $1\frac{1}{9}$ B $\frac{2}{3}$ C $\frac{10}{18}$ D $\frac{1}{3}$

6. $\frac{7}{10} - \frac{3}{10} = \frac{?}{}$

F 2 G $1\frac{3}{10}$ H 1 J $\frac{2}{5}$

7. One number is 5 more than 9. The other number is 19 less than 22. Find the prime factors of the product of the two numbers.

   A 6, 7

   B 2, 3, 7

   C 2, 21

   D 3, 10

8. Sheila is building bookshelves. She needs a board that is at least $1\frac{1}{2}$ in. thick. She has no boards that thick, so she decides to glue together two boards. Which pair of boards can she use?

   F a $\frac{3}{8}$-in. board and a $\frac{1}{8}$-in. board

   G a $\frac{1}{8}$-in. board and a $\frac{7}{8}$-in. board

   H a $\frac{3}{4}$-in. board and a $\frac{3}{4}$-in. board

   J a $\frac{1}{2}$-in. board and a $\frac{1}{2}$-in. board

9. **Write About It** Explain why you chose the answer you did for Problem 7.

Possible answer: I broke 42 down as 2 × 21. 2 is prime, but 21 can break

down as 7 × 3. 2, 3, and 7 are all prime, so they are the prime factors of 42.

Add and Subtract Mixed Numbers

Understand ➡ Plan ➡ Solve ➡ Check

Write the correct answer.

1. $2\frac{1}{8} + 3\frac{3}{8} = \underline{\ ?\ }$

$5\frac{4}{8}$, or $5\frac{1}{2}$

2. $5\frac{3}{5} - 4\frac{2}{5} = \underline{\ ?\ }$

$1\frac{1}{5}$

3. Neal eats $\frac{7}{8}$ of a pizza. Verne eats $\frac{6}{8}$ of a pizza. How much more pizza does Neal eat than Verne?

$\frac{1}{8}$ of a pizza more

4. Hilary finds 3 quarters in her jacket pocket. What fraction of a dollar does she have?

$\frac{3}{4}$ of a dollar

Choose the letter of the correct answer.

5. $8\frac{3}{4} - 2\frac{1}{4}$

A $6\frac{1}{2}$ **C** 9

B $6\frac{3}{4}$ **D** $11\frac{1}{2}$

6. $\frac{3}{9} + \frac{2}{9}$

F $\frac{2}{9}$ **H** $\frac{5}{9}$

G $\frac{5}{18}$ **J** $1\frac{4}{5}$

7. Wendy needs a $6\frac{1}{4}$-in. piece of trim. She has a box of smaller lengths of trim. Which pair of pieces can she put together to get the length she needs?

A $3\frac{3}{4}$-in. piece and $2\frac{3}{4}$-in. piece

B $4\frac{2}{4}$-in. piece and $1\frac{3}{4}$-in. piece

C 2-in. piece and $4\frac{3}{4}$-in. piece

D $3\frac{1}{4}$-in. piece and $2\frac{3}{4}$-in. piece

8. The sum of the digits of a 3-digit odd number is 13. The digit in the tens place is 4 less than the digit in the hundreds place and 3 more than the ones digit. What is the number?

F 625 **H** 841

G 733 **J** 952

9. Write About It How did you find the answer to Problem 7?

Possible answer: I added the mixed numbers in each choice to find the

total number of inches.

Understand Cause and Effect

Understand ➡ Plan ➡ Solve ➡ Check

A **cause** is the reason something happens. An **effect** is what happens as a result of the cause. A cause may have more than one effect. An effect may have more than one cause. Read the following problem.

VOCABULARY

cause

effect

> An ice storm caused power lines to fall down. As a result, only $\frac{1}{10}$ of the population in one town had power. The power company promised special emergency repairs if more than $\frac{1}{2}$ of the population lost power. What fraction of the population lost power? Will the power company make emergency repairs?

1. List the causes in the **Cause** column. List the effects in the **Effect** column. Possible answers are given.

Cause	Effect
ice storm	Power lines fell down. $\frac{9}{10}$ of population lost power.
Think: Did over one half of the population lose power? Yes, over $\frac{1}{2}$ of the population lost power.	Think: What will happen? Then the power company will make emergency repairs.

2. Solve the problem. $\frac{9}{10} > \frac{1}{2}$; yes, the power company will make emergency repairs.

3. Describe the strategy you used. Possible answer: I made a model to compare $\frac{1}{2}$ and $\frac{9}{10}$.

List a cause and an effect in each problem. Solve.

4. Mr. Bowers tells 8 students that if more than half lost power for at least 3 days, he will postpone the math test. In the group, $\frac{2}{8}$ lost power for 1 day. The rest lost power for 3 days. Will Mr. Bowers postpone the test?

Cause: More than half of the group lost power for more than 3 days. Effect: Mr. Bowers will postpone the test. Yes.

5. Ryan decided to do his homework by candlelight. Of the total time that he had, he spent $\frac{1}{5}$ doing math and $\frac{2}{5}$ doing science. The candles burned out before he had time to do English. What fraction of the time was left?

Cause: Candles burned out. Effect: He did not do English homework. $\frac{2}{5}$ of the time.

Add Unlike Fractions

Write the correct answer.

1. $8\frac{3}{8} + 2\frac{1}{8}$

$10\frac{1}{2}$

2. Write three fractions that are equivalent to $\frac{2}{3}$.

Possible answers $\frac{4}{6}, \frac{6}{9}, \frac{8}{12}$

3. $\frac{1}{6} + \frac{2}{3}$

$\frac{5}{6}$

4. Carolyn walked $\frac{2}{5}$ mile on Monday and $\frac{6}{10}$ mile on Wednesday. How far did Carolyn walk in all?

$\frac{10}{10}$, or 1 mile

Choose the letter of the correct answer.

5. Which pair shows *like* fractions?

A $\frac{1}{3}, \frac{1}{5}$ C $\frac{2}{5}, \frac{3}{5}$

B $\frac{1}{2}, \frac{1}{4}$ D $\frac{3}{6}, \frac{3}{7}$

6. Which is a prime factor of 40?

F 9   H 7

G 8   J 2

7. Veronica's dresser is $4\frac{2}{12}$ feet long. Her bed is $6\frac{5}{12}$ feet long. How much longer is her bed than her dresser?

A $10\frac{7}{12}$ feet   C $2\frac{1}{4}$ feet

B $8\frac{1}{2}$ feet   D $\frac{11}{3}$ feet

8. Serena must practice her clarinet each day. She practiced in the morning for $\frac{1}{4}$ hour and in the afternoon for $\frac{1}{3}$ hour. How long did Serena practice in all?

F $\frac{7}{12}$ hour   H $\frac{5}{12}$ hour

G $\frac{1}{2}$ hour   J $\frac{1}{3}$ hour

9. **Write About It** Explain your solution to Problem 8.

Possible answer: I used fraction bars to find the sum of $\frac{1}{4} + \frac{1}{3}$

I found the like fraction bars that together are equivalent to $\frac{1}{4} + \frac{1}{3}$ in

length. Seven $\frac{1}{12}$ fraction bars are equal in length to $\frac{1}{4} + \frac{1}{3}$.

Subtract Unlike Fractions

Understand → Plan → Solve → Check

Write the correct answer.

1. Use fraction bars to find the difference.

$$\frac{7}{10} - \frac{2}{5}$$

$$\frac{3}{10}$$

2. Add.

$$2\frac{1}{4} + 3\frac{3}{4}$$

$$5\frac{4}{4}, \text{ or } 6$$

3. A $2\frac{1}{3}$-yard length is cut off of a $5\frac{2}{3}$-yard strip of vinyl siding. What is the length of the remaining strip of siding?

$$3\frac{1}{3} \text{ yd}$$

4. A recipe calls for $\frac{3}{4}$ cup sugar. Emily has $\frac{1}{2}$ cup. How much sugar does she still need?

$$\frac{1}{4} \text{ c}$$

Choose the letter of the correct answer.

5. $\frac{1}{2} - \frac{1}{3}$

A $\frac{1}{6}$　　　　C $\frac{5}{6}$

B $\frac{1}{2}$　　　　D 1

6. $\frac{11}{12} - \frac{2}{3}$

F 1　　　　H $\frac{2}{3}$

G $\frac{3}{4}$　　　　J $\frac{1}{4}$

7. The gravity on the moon and some of the planets would make you weigh less than you weigh on Earth. Order the moon and the three planets from the one you would weigh the greatest on to the one you would weigh the least on.

	Moon	Pluto	Mercury	Mars
Fraction of Weight on Earth	$\frac{17}{100}$	$\frac{4}{100}$	$\frac{37}{100}$	$\frac{38}{100}$

A Moon, Pluto, Mercury, Mars
B Pluto, Moon, Mercury, Mars
C Mars, Mercury, Pluto, Moon
D Mars, Mercury, Moon, Pluto

8. Twelve grandchildren want to pay equal amounts to buy a gift for their grandparents' fiftieth wedding anniversary. For which gift would they be able to pay equal whole-dollar amounts?

F a $100 silver platter
G a $90 punch bowl
H an $84 sculpture
J a $77 painting

9. **Write About It** Explain how you chose your answer to Problem 8.

Possible answer: If 12 grandchildren want to pay equal whole-dollar amounts, the cost must be a multiple of 12. Of the choices, only 84 is a multiple of 12.

Record Outcomes

Write the correct answer.

1. How many possible outcomes are there for tossing a coin and tossing a cube labeled 1 to 6?

   _____ 12 outcomes _____

2. Donna and Alex toss a 2-color counter colored yellow and red, and spin the pointer on a spinner labeled 1, 2, 3, and 4. List the possible outcomes of this experiment.

   _ Y1, Y2, Y3, Y4, R1, R2, R3, R4 _

3. Write $<$, $>$, or $=$ in the $\bigcirc$.

   $10 \times (4 \times 2) \; \overline{>} \; 3 \times (6 \times 2)$

4. Find the value of the variable in

   $11 \times n = 121$

   _____ $n = 11$ _____

Choose the letter of the correct answer.

5. How many possible outcomes are there when you toss a coin and spin the pointer on a spinner with 3 colors?

   A 4   **C** 12
   B 6   **D** 18

6. $253,647 - 36,988 = \blacksquare$

   F 216,649   **H** 216,699
   G 216,659   **J** 226,679

7. On Monday, Russell and his grandfather gathered 16 eggs; on Tuesday, 21 eggs; on Wednesday, 27 eggs and on Thursday, 12 eggs. What is the average number of eggs they gathered?

   A 27 eggs   **C** 17 eggs
   B 19 eggs   **D** 12 eggs

8. Thomas tossed a coin and spun the pointer on a spinner with 4 colors (blue, green, red, and yellow). How many different outcomes are there?

   F 6   **H** 9
   G 8   **J** 12

9. **Write About It** Explain how you got your answer for Problem 8.

   Possible answer: I made a table listing all the possible outcomes for

   heads and for tails and the four colors. There were eight outcomes

   altogether.

Name _____

Predict Outcomes of Experiments

Understand ➡ Plan ➡ Solve ➡ Check

Write the correct answer.

1. Write *likely* or *unlikely* to describe landing on blue when spinning the pointer on a spinner that has 4 equal sections colored blue, yellow, red, and green.

unlikely

2. Write *likely*, *unlikely*, or *equally likely* to describe tossing a 3 or a 5 on a number cube labeled 1–6.

equally likely

3. List all the possible outcomes of tossing a coin and a cube labeled 1–6.

H1, H2, H3, H4, H5, H6,

T1, T2, T3, T4, T5, T6

4. Which type of graph would be best to show the number of children in each of the houses in your neighborhood?

bar graph

Choose the letter of the correct answer.

5. If you spin the pointer 20 times, on which number is it most likely to stop?

A 5
B 10
C 15
D 20

6. Which type of graph would be best to show how much you have grown over the past five years?

F line graph
G line plot
H bar graph
J stem-and-leaf plot

7. Toni is 5 years older than Fran. Fran is twice as old as Ann Marie. Ann Marie is 5 years old. How old is Toni?

A 15 yr   C 8 yr
B 10 yr   D 6 yr

8. If you toss a number cube labeled 1–6, how likely is it that you will toss a composite number?

F certain   H unlikely
G likely   J impossible

9. **Write About It**   Describe how you solved Problem 7.

Possible answer: Ann Marie is 5 years old, so I multiplied

5 × 2 to find Fran's age. Then I added 5 to find Toni's age.

Probability as a Fraction

Understand ➡ Plan ➡ Solve ➡ Check

Write the correct answer.

1. Write a fraction for the probability of the pointer on this spinner stopping on an odd number.

$\frac{3}{5}$

2. Write a fraction for the probability of the pointer on the spinner in Problem 1 stopping on an even number.

$\frac{2}{5}$

3. How many different outfits can be made with 4 shirts and 2 pairs of pants?

8 outfits

4. Divide.

$7\overline{)3,921}$

560r1

Choose the letter of the correct answer.

5. Which fraction shows the probability of getting a 7 when you toss a cube labeled 1–6?

A $\frac{0}{6}$ C $\frac{1}{6}$

B $\frac{1}{7}$ D $\frac{7}{6}$

6. Which fraction shows the probability of getting an odd number when you toss a cube labeled 1–6?

F $\frac{1}{3}$ H $\frac{1}{2}$

G $\frac{2}{6}$ J $\frac{5}{6}$

7. Violette has an appointment in the city at 3:00 P.M. To get there, she takes a train and then a subway. The subway ride will take 20 minutes. The train ride will take 50 minutes. Which train should she take if she wants to get to her appointment early?

A the 1:25 P.M.   C the 2:05 P.M.
B the 1:55 P.M.   D the 11:25 P.M.

8. **Write About It** Explain how you chose your answer for Problem 5.

Possible answer: Since the cube does not have a 7, there are 0 ways to toss it. In the fraction $\frac{0}{6}$, the 0 shows the number of ways to toss a 7, and the 6 shows the number of events that could happen.

More About Probability

Write the correct answer.

1. $n \div 6 = 12$

$n = 72$

2. Taylor is going to pull a letter from the alphabet out of a bag of cards. What is the probability that the letter will be a vowel?

$\frac{5}{26}$

3. Alex has a spinner with 5 equal parts labeled 1, 2, 3, 4, and 5. After 10 spins, the pointer had stopped on 3 four times. Based on the experiment, write the probability of spinning a 3.

$\frac{4}{10}$, or $\frac{2}{5}$

4. Lelah and 12 other children write their names on pieces of paper and put them in a hat. If Jon pulls a name out of the hat, what is the probability that Lelah's name will be pulled?

$\frac{1}{13}$

Choose the letter of the correct answer.

5. Tina has a bag of marbles with 6 red, 3 green, and 4 yellow marbles. She pulls a marble from the bag without looking at it. What is the mathematical probability of pulling a red marble from the bag?

A $\frac{6}{12}$ C $\frac{4}{13}$

B $\frac{6}{13}$ D $\frac{3}{13}$

6. Vivian has a spinner with 8 equal sections. Three of the sections are red and 2 of the sections are green. Blue, yellow, and orange each have one section. What is the probability of spinning green?

F $\frac{1}{2}$ H $\frac{1}{4}$

G $\frac{3}{8}$ J $\frac{1}{8}$

7. Tyree tossed a coin 100 times and got 70 heads. How does her probability compare to the mathematical probability?

A It is less.   C They are equal.

B It is more.   D can't tell

8. Which is a reasonable outcome for the number of heads if a coin is tossed 300 times?

F 100   H 200

G 157   J 270

9. Write About It Explain your answer to Problem 7.

Possible answer: Tyree got a probability of $\frac{7}{10}$, which is greater than $\frac{1}{2}$.

Understand ➡ Plan ➡ Solve ➡ Check

Combinations

Write the correct answer.

1. Joy has a choice of 3 different colors of paint (white, brown, and green) along with 2 types of border patterns (birds, flowers). How many different looking rooms can she make with one paint color and one border pattern?

6 rooms

2. Nina has a choice of 4 different sandwich spreads (tuna salad, chicken salad, ham salad, and egg salad) along with 3 types of breads (white, whole wheat, and rye). How many different sandwiches could she make?

12 sandwiches

3. Hector is packing for a trip. He packs 4 shirts and 5 pairs of shorts. How many different outfits can he make?

20 outfits

4. What type of triangle has sides with different lengths?

scalene triangle

Choose the letter of the correct answer.

5. Find the number of clothing choices:

Shoes: black, brown, gray
Socks: black, brown, beige

A 18   **C** 9
B 12   **D** 6

6. Write six million seven hundred fifty-three thousand, one hundred forty-four in standard form.

F 735,144
G 6,753,144
H 7,653,144
J 7,735,134

7. How many different outfits can Katrina make from these choices?

Sweaters: blue, green, tan, white
Slacks: navy, black, brown

A 6   **C** 12
B 9   **D** 18

8. Which fracion shows the probability of getting a number greater than 2 when you toss a cube labeled 1–6?

F $\frac{3}{6}$ **H** $\frac{5}{6}$
G $\frac{2}{3}$ **J** 1

9. Write About It Explain how you determined the number of outfits in Problem 7.

Possible answer: I made a tree diagram with blue, green, white, and tan as the first branches. Then I added navy, black, and brown to each branch. This made 12 choices.

© Harcourt

Understand ➡ Plan ➡ Solve ➡ Check

Classify and Categorize

When a problem involves a great deal of information, it is helpful to classify and categorize the information.

To *classify* information means to group together information that is related.

To *categorize* information means to put a label on those groups.

> The Garcias are building a new house. They can choose among tan, blue, gray, and white for the color of the siding. The shutters can be either black, green, or red. They can also choose siding or shutters in maroon. The trim can be either white or cream.

Use a table to help classify and categorize the information. Fill in the missing information.

SIDING	Shutters	TRIM
tan	black	white
blue	green	cream
gray	red	
white	maroon	
maroon		

← Categories

Classify, or group together, information that is related.

1. Name 2 choices of siding, shutters, and trim.

   Possible answer: white siding, black shutters, white trim;

   gray siding, red shutters, cream trim

Classify and categorize to solve.

2. Teri is decorating cakes. She makes green icing and white roses and buys yellow and blue icing and pink and red roses. How many different ways can Teri decorate a cake?

   9

3. The parents are having an ice cream sundae party. Mrs. Wong brings vanilla and chocolate ice cream and caramel topping. Mr. Petty brings strawberry ice cream and fudge topping. How many different sundaes can be made?

   6

Name _____

Length: Choose the Appropriate Unit

Write the correct answer.

1. Choose the most reasonable unit of measure. The distance from your town to the state line is 37 __?__.

_____
mi

2. Order $\frac{2}{3}$, $\frac{1}{2}$, $\frac{1}{4}$, and $\frac{7}{8}$ from *greatest* to *least*.

$\frac{7}{8}$ $\frac{2}{3}$ $\frac{1}{2}$ $\frac{1}{4}$
_____

3. Write the most reasonable unit of measure. The distance a football player carried the ball down the field was 21 __?__.

_____
yd

4. What is the next fraction in the pattern? $\frac{1}{4}$, $\frac{2}{8}$, $\frac{3}{12}$, $\frac{4}{16}$, $\cdots$

$\frac{5}{20}$
_____

Choose the letter of the correct answer.

5. Add.

$$2\frac{3}{8} + 5\frac{1}{8}$$

A $7\frac{4}{7}$ C $7\frac{1}{4}$

B $7\frac{1}{2}$ D $6\frac{5}{8}$

6. Which unit would be the most reasonable one to use to measure the amount of rain that falls in one month?

F in. G ft H yd J mi

7. Which is the longest measurement?

A 322 in.
B 322 yd
C 322 ft
D 322 mi

8. Scott is setting up a display in a grocery store. He needs to stack equal rows of cans. Which arrangement uses the most cans?

F 4 rows of 12 cans
G 3 rows of 10 cans
H 5 rows of 10 cans
J 2 rows of 15 cans

9. **Write About It** Explain your solution for Problem 8.

Possible answer: For each answer choice I multiplied by the number of

cans in each row by the number of rows. 5 rows of 10 cans has the

greatest product.

_____

© Harcourt

Measure Fractional Parts

Write the correct answer.

1. Estimate the length of the screw to the nearest inch.

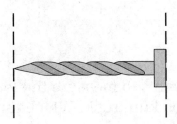

1 or 2 in.

2. Measure the length of the clip to the nearest $\frac{1}{4}$ inch.

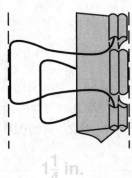

$1\frac{1}{4}$ in.

3. William measures the height of his 2-year-old brother to see how much he has grown. Which unit of measure should he use?

in. or ft

4. In the long jump, Jason jumped $144\frac{1}{4}$ in., $144\frac{5}{8}$ in., and $144\frac{1}{2}$ in. The judges count the jump that is the greatest distance. Which jump did the judges count?

$144\frac{5}{8}$ in.

Choose the letter of the correct answer.

5. Subtract. $4\frac{7}{8} - 3\frac{1}{8}$

   A 1

   B $1\frac{1}{4}$

   C $1\frac{2}{4}$

   D $1\frac{3}{4}$

6. Which is the measure of the clip in Problem 2 to the nearest $\frac{1}{2}$ in.?

   F 1 in.

   G $1\frac{1}{2}$ in.

   H 2 in.

   J $2\frac{1}{2}$ in.

7. If February 29 falls on a Friday in one year, which day of the week will April 1 fall on in that year?

   A Monday   C Wednesday
   B Tuesday   D Thursday

8. Henry measured a length of wood as 7 inches to the nearest inch. Which of the following lengths could *not* be the one Henry measured?

   F $6\frac{3}{4}$ in.   H $7\frac{5}{8}$ in.

   G $7\frac{3}{8}$ in.   J $6\frac{7}{8}$ in.

9. **Write About It** What are the longest and the shortest lengths that could be labeled "7 inches to the nearest inch"?

Possible answer: Any length $6\frac{1}{2}$ in. or greater and less than $7\frac{1}{2}$ in.

measures 7 in. when measured to the nearest inch.

© Harcourt

Algebra: Change Linear Units

Understand → Plan → Solve → Check

Write the correct answer.

1. Complete.

   48 in. = _____4_____ ft

2. Complete.

   2 mi = ____10,560____ ft

3. Jocelyn wants to measure the size of her computer screen. Which unit of measure should she use?

   _____in._____

4. Brad wants to measure the length of his pickup truck. Which unit of measure should he use?

   _____ft or yd_____

Choose the letter of the correct answer.

5. Which word makes the sentence true?

   To change from yd to mi, you __?__.

   A add   C multiply
   B subtract   D divide

6. Which measurement is equivalent to 360 in.?

   F 10 yd   H 36 ft
   G 30 yd   J 100 yd

7. The distance from Earth to the moon is about 250,000 miles. The distance from Earth to the sun is about 400 times the distance from Earth to the moon. Estimate the distance from Earth to the sun.

   A About 250,000,000 mi
   B About 150,000,000 mi
   C About 100,000,000 mi
   D About 100,000 mi

8. What is the remainder when 482 is divided by 7?

   F 3
   G 5
   H 6
   J 9

9. **Write About It** Explain the steps you took to solve Problem 7.

   Possible answer: The distance from Earth to the Sun is about

   250,000 × 400, or 100,000,000, mi.

Capacity

Write the correct answer.

1. Complete.

   4 gal = __?__ qt

   _____ 16 _____

2. Complete.

   8 cups = __?__ pt

   _____ 4 _____

3. Carol has a $2\frac{3}{4}$-hour radio show. There are $1\frac{1}{4}$ hours just for music. The rest are devoted to talk. How many hours of Carol's show are devoted to talk?

   _____ $1\frac{1}{2}$ hr _____

4. On Tuesday, Jean runs 3 miles on the school track. Philippe runs 8,000 yards. How much farther does Philippe run?

   _____ 2,720 yd or 8,160 ft _____

Choose the letter of the correct answer.

5. Which is the greatest measurement of capacity?

   A 2 gal   **C** 2 pt
   B 2 qt   **D** 2 c

6. Which measurement is equal to 4 quarts?

   F 2 c   **H** 1 gal
   G 16 pt   **J** 32 c

7. Ray and Bob are driving 1,200 miles by car. They drive at an average speed of 60 miles per hour. How long will the drive take?

   A 18 hr
   B 19 hr
   C 20 hr
   D 25 hr

8. Connie's new car gets 32 miles per gallon of gasoline. About how many miles can Connie drive per quart of gasoline?

   F 2 mi
   G 4 mi
   H 8 mi
   J 16 mi

9. **Write About It** Explain the steps you took to solve Problem 6.

   Possible answer: I made a mental image of 4 quarts and compared

   it to all 4 choices. Only 1 gal has the same capacity as 4 quarts.

   _____

   _____

   _____

Name _____

Weight

Write the correct answer.

Understand → Plan → Solve → Check

1. Choose the most reasonable unit of measure. Write *oz*, *lb*, or *T*.

lb

2. Choose the most reasonable unit of measure. Write *oz*, *lb*, or *T*.

BUTTER

oz

3. Dave needs 4 cups of whipping cream for a pie. The store sells whipping cream in 1-pint containers. How many pints should Dave buy?

2 pt

4. Lucy needs to fill up a large washtub so she can give her Great Dane a bath. She wants to know the capacity of the washtub. What unit of measure should she use?

gal

Choose the letter of the correct answer.

5. How many pounds are in 3 tons?

A 2,000 lb   C 600 lb
B 6,000 lb   D 6,000 oz

6. How many pounds are in 64 ounces?

F 2 lb   G 4 lb   H 6 lb   J 8 lb

7. Chas has 6 coins in his pocket. Which amount could *not* be the total value of his 6 coins?

A $0.10
B $0.15
C $0.20
D $1.50

8. A riddle asks, "Which weighs more: a ton of bricks, or a ton of feathers?" Suppose a brick weighs 1 lb. Together, 20 feathers weigh about 1 oz. About how many more feathers than bricks would you need to have 1 T?

F about 160 times as many
G about 200 times as many
H about 320 times as many
J about 1,600 times as many

9. **Write About It** Describe the method you used to solve Problem 8.

Possible answer: Find the number of feathers in 1 lb: 20 per oz × 16 oz = about 320 per lb. So the number of feathers in 1 T is about 320 times the number of bricks.

© Harcourt

Sequence Information

Understand ➡ Plan ➡ Solve ➡ Check

A **sequence** is an arrangement of one thing after another. You can use sequence clues to determine the order of events in a problem. Look for words such as *first*, *last*, *next*, *then*, *now*, *before*, *after*, and *already*. Read the following problem.

VOCABULARY
sequence

> Henry made a coat rack from a board. He placed the first peg 4 in. from the left end. He placed the last peg 4 in. from the right end. He also placed 1 peg every 4 in. between the end pegs. The board he used was already cut to 3 ft long. How many pegs did he use?

1. Underline the sequence clues below. Then list each event in the order in which it happened.

Sequence Clues	Order of Events
He placed the first peg 4 in. from the left end.	He had a 3-ft piece of wood.
He placed the last peg 4 in. from the right end.	He placed a peg 4 in. from the left end.
He placed 1 peg every 4 in.	He placed a peg 4 in. from the right end.
The board he used was already cut to 3 ft.	He placed 1 peg every 4 in.

2. Solve the problem. _____ 8 pegs _____

3. Describe the strategy you used. _____ Possible answer: I drew a diagram. _____

Underline the sequence clues in each problem. Solve.

4. Lenore hung paintings on one wall in the art gallery. After she measured the wall and found it to be 8 yd, she hung the first picture 6 ft from the left end of the wall. Then she hung 1 painting every 6 ft. The last thing she did was hang a painting 6 ft from the right end of the wall. How many paintings did Lenore hang?

_____ 3 paintings _____

5. Howard made a long banner with flags from different countries. After cutting out a 4-ft-long piece of cloth for the banner, he glued the first flag 6 in. from the left end. Next he glued 1 flag every 6 in. He glued the last flag 6 in. from the right end. How many flags did Howard glue onto the banner?

_____ 7 flags _____

Name _____

Metric Length

Understand ➡ Plan ➡ Solve ➡ Check

Write the correct answer.

1. Choose the most reasonable unit to measure the length of a baseball field. Write *mm, cm, dm,* or *m.*

   _____ m _____

2. Choose the most reasonable unit to measure the width of a computer disk. Write *mm, cm, dm,* or *m.*

   _____ cm _____

3. Ty says that his new baby sister weighs 128 ounces. Write his sister's weight in pounds.

   _____ 8 lb _____

4. Melanie is 48 inches tall. Write Melanie's height in feet.

   _____ 4 ft _____

Choose the letter of the correct answer.

5. Which measurement is about the length of your desk?

   A 10 cm   **C** 100 dm
   B 100 cm   **D** 1,000 dm

6. Which measurement is equivalent to 15,840 feet?

   F 2 mi   **H** 1,760 yd
   G 3 mi   **J** 3,520 yd

7. The heights of the 5 starting players on the basketball team are 73 inches, 76 inches, 64 inches, 69 inches, and 78 inches. What is their average height in feet?

   A 5 ft   **C** 6 ft
   B $5\frac{1}{2}$ ft   **D** $6\frac{1}{2}$ ft

8. A book with 28 chapters has an average of 16 pages per chapter. The book also has 12 pages in the front and an index of 8 pages. Which expression could you use to find the total number of pages in the book?

   F $28 \times (16 + 12 + 8)$
   G $28 \times (16 + 8) + 12$
   H $(28 \times 16) + 12 + 8$
   J $(28 \times 16) \times 12 + 8$

9. **Write About It** Describe how you decided whether to multiply or divide in Problems 3 and 4.

   Possible answer: I compared the sizes of the units: in both problems,

   I had to change a smaller unit to a larger one, which meant there would

   be fewer of the new unit. So, to get fewer units, I knew I would have

   to divide.

© Harcourt

Algebra: Change Linear Units

Write the correct answer.

1. Write the number you would multiply by to change meters to decimeters.

$$dm = \blacksquare \times m$$

10

2. Write the number that makes the measures equivalent.

$$18 \text{ dm} = \blacksquare \text{ cm}$$

180

3. Sonia's dad is 200 centimeters tall. How many meters tall is he?

2 m

4. Diane knows her family's pickup truck can carry a load of as much as 2 tons. How many pounds is this?

4,000 lb

Choose the letter of the correct answer.

5. Which measure is equivalent to 37 decimeters?

   A 3.7 cm
   B 370 cm
   C 370 m
   D 3,700 cm

6. Which measure is equivalent to 420 meters?

   F 4,200 cm
   G 42,000 cm
   H 42 dm
   J 420 dm

7. Pedro has one dollar more than Kate. Patti has $5 less than Kate. They have $20 in all. How much money does Kate have?

   A $3
   B $5
   C $8
   D $10

8. Jon has scores of 88, 92, 81, 98, and 86 on his math tests. What is Jon's median score?

   F 81
   G 88
   H 89
   J 92

9. **Write About It** Describe the steps you took to solve Problem 8.

   Possible answer: I ordered all of Jon's scores from least to greatest and
   then I found the middle score of 88.

Capacity

Write the correct answer.

1. Choose the more reasonable unit for measuring the capacity of a coffee mug. Write *mL* or *L*.

   mL

2. Choose the more reasonable unit for measuring the capacity of a punch bowl. Write *mL* or *L*.

   L

3. Joy estimates that her dripping bathtub faucet would take only 1 day to fill the bathtub. She wants to estimate how much water that is. Choose the most reasonable unit for measuring capacity. Write *cup*, *quart*, or *gallon*.

   gal

4. Brian is school champion in the 100-meter dash. He wants to know how many centimeters are in 100 meters. Find the answer for Brian.

   10,000 cm

Choose the letter of the correct answer.

5. What is the most reasonable measurement for the capacity of a goldfish bowl?

   A 2 L   C 200 mL
   B 20 L   D 20 mL

6. What is the most reasonable measurement for the capacity of a car's gasoline tank?

   F 4 L   H 40 mL
   G 40 L   J 400 mL

7. Brandon opens a bottle of apple juice and drinks 8 oz of it. He pours the same amount into a pot of applesauce he is making. His sister then drinks 4 oz of the juice and pours a 4-oz glass for their mother. Brandon and his father each drink a 4-oz glass. How many ounces of juice did they use?

   A 32 oz   C 96 oz
   B 40 oz   D 128 oz

8. What is the next number in the pattern?

   12, 24, 36, 48, 60, 72, ▪

   F 68   H 84
   G 74   J 192

9. **Write About It** Describe the strategy you used to solve Problem 7.

   Possible answer: I added the 8 oz that Brandon drank to the 8 oz he poured

   into the applesauce to get 16 oz. Then, I multiplied 4 oz by 4 for each glass of

   juice that the family drank to get 16 oz. Finally I added the totals to get 32 oz.

Mass

Understand ➡ Plan ➡ Solve ➡ Check

Write the correct answer.

1. Sandy is a star basketball player. Which is the more reasonable unit to measure his mass: 110 g or 110 kg?

_____110 kg_____

2. Ms. Masters likes to sew dresses. Which is the more reasonable unit to measure the mass of her sewing needle: 500 mg or 500 g?

_____500 mg_____

3. Charles is the state javelin champion. Which is the most reasonable unit to measure the length of his best throw: mm, cm, m, or km?

_____m_____

4. Nikita finds a broken spring in the wrist watch she is repairing. Which is the most reasonable unit to measure the length of the spring: mm, m, or km?

_____mm_____

Choose the letter of the correct answer.

5. Which is the most reasonable unit to measure the mass of a pickup truck?

A mg   B g   C kg   D km

6. Which is the most reasonable unit to measure the mass of a flute?

F mg   G g   H kg   J cm

7. A cheer starts, "Two bits, four bits, six bits, a dollar." If a dollar is worth 8 bits, what coin is worth two bits?

A nickel
B dime
C quarter
D half-dollar

8. Wesley needs to move 820 kg of grain across the river in a canoe that can carry no more than 120 kg. Wesley has a mass of 70 kg. What is the fewest number of trips he will have to make?

F 17 trips   H 32 trips
G 18 trips   J 33 trips

9. **Write About It** Explain how you got your answer to Problem 8.

Possible answer: I subtracted 70 kg from 120 kg to get 50 kg, the amount of

grain the canoe could carry on each crossing. Then I divided 820 by 50 to get

16 round trips, or 32 crossings, with a remainder of 20 kg for 1 final crossing.

Make Inferences

Understand ➡ Plan ➡ Solve ➡ Check

To **make inferences** means to draw conclusions based on the given information. In order to make an inference, you must examine all of the given information. Read the following problem.

VOCABULARY

make
inferences

> In the morning, Mary and Billy each caught one fish. Mary's fish measured 9 decimeters and Billy's fish measured 1 meter. In the afternoon, Mary caught another fish. Mary caught the longest fish of the day. What inference can you make about the fish that Mary caught in the afternoon?

1. Examine the information given in the problem. Then make inferences about that information.

Information	Inference
Length of Mary's first fish is ___9 dm___. Length of Billy's fish is ___1 m___. Length of Mary's second fish is unknown. Mary caught the longest fish.	Possible answer: The lengths need to be compared in the same units before inferring anything about Mary's second fish.
Mary's first fish is ___90___ cm long. Billy's fish is ___100___ cm long.	Possible answer: Since Billy's fish is longer than Mary's first fish, Mary's second fish must be longer than Billy's fish.

2. Solve the problem. _Mary's first fish is 90 cm; Billy's fish is_

   100 cm; Mary's second fish must be longer than 100 cm.

3. Describe the strategy you used. _Possible answer: I solved a simpler problem._

Make inferences to solve.

4. Stan and Tomiko raced toy cars. In the first trial, Stan's car went 18 decimeters and Tomiko's car went 110 centimeters. In the second trial, Stan's car went 110 centimeters and Tomiko's car went the longest distance out of the two trials. What inference can you make about the second trial?

   Possible answer: Tomiko's car went more than 180 cm in the

   second trial.

Relate Benchmark Measurements

Write the correct answer.

1. Is one foot greater than or less than one meter?

_____ less than _____

2. Travis has a piece of wood that is 2 feet long. He cuts off a piece that is $1\frac{1}{4}$ feet long. How much wood is left?

$\frac{3}{4}$ ft

3. There are 235 beads in each container. The teacher buys 6 containers for arts and crafts. How many beads are there in all?

_____ 1,410 beads _____

4. Camilla walked 2 miles. Did she walk more than or less than 2 kilometers? Explain.

_____ more, since a mile is longer _____

_____ than a kilometer _____

Choose the letter of the correct answer.

5. Which comparison is false?

A 4 in. > 4 cm   **C** 1 qt < 1 L
B 2 kg < 2 lb   **D** 3 m > 3 yd

6. Jessie drank $\frac{1}{2}$ liter of water. How many milliliters of water did she drink?

F 5 mL   **H** 500 mL
G 50 mL   **J** 5,000 mL

7. About how many ounces are equivalent to 60 grams?

A 2 ounces
B 10 ounces
C 60 ounces
D 100 ounces

8. Michael ran 1,200 meters, Kelly ran 1,800 meters, and Ralph ran twice as many meters as Michael ran. How many meters did Ralph run?

F 600 meters   **H** 2,400 meters
G 900 meters   **J** 3,600 meters

9. Write About It Explain how you solved Problem 1.

Possible answer: 1 meter is a little longer than 1 yard, so 1 yd < 1m

and 1 ft < 1 yd, so 1 ft < 1m.

Name _____

Relate Fractions and Decimals

Write the correct answer.

1. Write the decimal and the fraction for the part that is shaded.

0.44, $\frac{44}{100}$

2. Write the decimal and the fraction for the part that is shaded.

0.74, $\frac{74}{100}$

3. In Mrs. Valerio's class, $\frac{2}{3}$ of the students bring lunch and $\frac{1}{3}$ of the students buy lunch at school. Which is greater—the fraction of the students that brings lunch or the fraction of the students that buys lunch?

the fraction that brings lunch

4. In a survey, $\frac{3}{10}$ of the people interviewed said they liked their jobs a great deal. Another $\frac{2}{10}$ said they liked their jobs somewhat. What was the total fraction of those interviewed who liked their jobs?

$\frac{5}{10}$, or $\frac{1}{2}$

Choose the letter of the correct answer.

5. Add. $\frac{1}{3} + \frac{3}{4} = \underline{\ ?\ }$

A $\frac{4}{9}$ **B** $\frac{4}{7}$ **C** $1\frac{1}{12}$ **D** $1\frac{3}{7}$

6. Which fraction is equivalent to the decimal 0.24?

F $\frac{2}{4}$ **G** $\frac{240}{100}$ **H** $\frac{24}{10}$ **J** $\frac{24}{100}$

7. Mike draws a square with a line connecting 2 opposite corners. Then he draws another line connecting the other pair of opposite corners. How many triangles are there in Mike's square?

A 2 triangles **C** 6 triangles
B 4 triangles **D** 8 triangles

8. Jill and Kate have $0.60. Jill says they have 0.6 dollar. Kate says they have $\frac{3}{5}$ dollar. Who is right?

F Jill **H** Kate
G Both **J** Neither

9. Write About It Explain the strategy you used to solve Problem 7.

Possible answer: I drew a model; then I copied it a few times so I could shade all of the different triangles I saw in the square because some of them overlapped.

© Harcourt

Decimals to Thousandths

Write the correct answer.

1. Write the number in word form.

Ones	.	Tenths	Hundredths	Thousandths
0	.	0	5	6

_____fifty-six thousandths_____

2. Write a number that has a 3 in the thousandths place, a 2 in the hundredths place, and a 0 in the tenths place.

_____Possible answer: 0.023_____

3. A band has 72 members and needs to buy 12 sheets of music for each member. How many sheets does it need to buy?

_____864 sheets_____

4. Jane spent $22.50 at the store. She gave the cashier $30.00. How much change did Jane get back?

_____$7.50_____

Choose the letter of the correct answer.

5. Which decimal is equivalent to $\frac{100}{1,000}$?

A 0.001   (C) 0.100

B 0.002   D 0.101

6. Which fraction is equivalent to 0.073?

F $\frac{73}{1}$ H $\frac{73}{100}$

G $\frac{73}{10}$ (J) $\frac{73}{1,000}$

7. Bob walked 0.6 mile to school. Ed walked $\frac{5}{10}$ mile to school. Who walked farther?

_____Bob_____

8. Lisa had some quarters in her bank. She added 6 dimes and then had a total of $1.35. How much money did she have in quarters?

_____$0.75_____

9. Write About It Explain the choice you made in Problem 6.

_____Possible answer: The digit 3 is in the thousandths place so 1,000 is_____

_____the denominator._____

Equivalent Decimals

Understand ➡ Plan ➡ Solve ➡ Check

Write the correct answer.

1. Write a decimal which is equivalent to 0.6.

   Possible answer: 0.60

2. Write $3\frac{1}{2}$ as a decimal.

   3.5

3. Marlee picked 0.3 pound of blackberries. Write an equivalent decimal for this amount.

   0.30

4. Solve. $9\frac{7}{8} - 1\frac{1}{8}$

   $8\frac{3}{4}$

Choose the letter of the correct answer.

5. Which pair of decimals is **not** equivalent?

   A 0.40 and 0.4

   B 0.05 and 0.50

   C 0.90 and 0.9

   D 0.3 and 0.3

6. Mariah's fish tank holds 30.5 gallons of water. Which is **not** equivalent to this amount?

   F 30.05 gallons

   G $30\frac{5}{10}$ gallons

   H 30.50 gallons

   J $30\frac{1}{2}$ gallons

7. Paul went to the toy store 5 times last month. Each time he bought 4 baseball cards for $2.00 each. Which operations could be used to find the total amount of money Paul spent?

   A addition or multiplication

   B addition or subtraction

   C division or addition

   D multiplication or subtraction

8. Koko's test scores last year were 89, 80, 81, 90, 99, 92 and 81. What was her median test score?

   F 81

   G 89

   H 90

   J 92

9. **Write About It** Explain your choice for Problem 7.   Possible answer: Paul buys the same thing 4 times, so I know I could use either repeated addition or multiplication. None of the other choices makes sense, since they include subtraction and division, and nothing is being taken away or divided into groups.

© Harcourt

Relate Mixed Numbers and Decimals

Write the correct answer.

1. Write a mixed number and decimal for the shaded part.

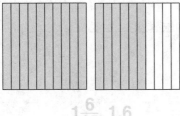

$1\frac{6}{10}$, 1.6

2. Write a mixed number and decimal for the shaded part.

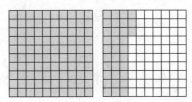

$1\frac{33}{100}$; 1.33

3. A library has 10 bookcases. Each has 10 shelves in it, all the same size. Out of all of the shelves in the library, 21 hold fiction. Write a decimal to show the part of the shelves that hold fiction.

0.21

4. Leo's famous chocolate chip cookie recipe calls for $2\frac{1}{2}$ cups of flour. Leo finds he has only $1\frac{1}{2}$ cups of flour. How much more flour will he need to get to make the cookies?

1 cup more

Choose the letter of the correct answer.

5. Which decimal is equivalent to $3\frac{3}{4}$?

   A 3.25   **B** 3.5   **C** 3.75   **D** 9.75

6. Which fraction is equivalent to 10.60?

   F $\frac{10}{6}$ **G** $10\frac{6}{100}$ **H** $10\frac{3}{5}$ **J** $10\frac{6}{5}$

7. Gina's family moves into a new home on a 7-acre lot. The lot is in a 100-acre development. Which decimal shows what part of the 100-acre development Gina's new lot is?

   A 0.007   **C** 0.7
   B 0.07   **D** 7.00

8. James leaves his house at 8:45 A.M. to go walking. He walks steadily at about 4 miles an hour and gets back home at 10:15 A.M. About how far has he walked?

   F about 4 mi   **H** about 6 mi
   G about 5 mi   **J** about 10 mi

9. **Write About It** Explain why you chose the answer you did for Problem 7.

   Possible answer: 7 acres out of 100 is $\frac{7}{100}$. That's equivalent to 0.07.

Compare and Order Decimals

Write the correct answer.

1. Write $>$, $<$, or $=$ to compare the two decimals.

0.33 0.3

_____ $>$ _____

2. Order the decimals 0.71, 0.81, 0.73, 0.8, and 0.7 from *least* to *greatest*. Use the number line.

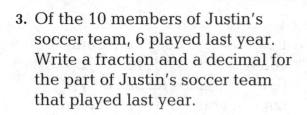

0.7   0.8   0.9   1.0

0.7, 0.71, 0.73, 0.8, 0.81

3. Of the 10 members of Justin's soccer team, 6 played last year. Write a fraction and a decimal for the part of Justin's soccer team that played last year.

$\frac{6}{10}$; 0.6

4. Krista spends $3\frac{1}{4}$ hours building a wall unit out of oak and another $4\frac{3}{4}$ hours applying finish to it. How many hours does she spend on the wall unit altogether?

8 hr

Choose the letter of the correct answer.

5. Which decimal is the greatest number?

A 0.02   C 0.2

B 0.20   D 0.22

6. Which group of decimals is ordered from *greatest* to *least*?

F 0.38, 0.49, 0.4, 0.39

G 0.352, 0.45, 0.416, 0.442

H 0.22, 0.38, 0.3, 0.4

J 0.451, 0.43, 0.318, 0.30

7. Mr. Morrel bought a package of 90 picture hangers. He is hanging 13 pictures which require 4 hangers each. How many hangers will he have left over?

A 38   C 48

B 40   D 52

8. Jeremy's friend Lena names four random numbers. The numbers are all decimals between 0 and 1. Which of the four decimals is least?

F 0.283   H 0.16

G 0.4   J 0.094

9. Write About It Describe the steps you took to solve Problem 7.

Possible answer: First, I found the number of hangers needed, 13 × 4 = 52.

Then I subtracted that number from the total, 90 − 52 = 38.

Text Format

Understand ➡ Plan ➡ Solve ➡ Check

Sometimes the way that text is arranged on a page can help you see the important information. The way the information is arranged is called **text format**.

VOCABULARY
text format

A speaker is coming to speak to Bobby's scout troop. The speaker has prepared some notes for his speech. Bobby looks at the notes and uses the *text format*, or the way the words are organized, to get information about the speech.

What will the speech be about?

The Most Important Things about Camping

Equipment
- a good tent
- good cooking supplies
- a place to put garbage

Safety
- know how to **SAFELY** put out a fire
- be aware of wildlife that could harm people
- be aware of plants that could harm people

Skills
- know how to build and light a fire
- know how to put up and take down a tent
- know how to tie knots

Bobby can see from the title of the notes that the speech will be about the most important things about camping.

---

1. How many categories of important things will the speaker be talking about? What are they?

   3; the speaker will be talking about equipment, safety, and skills.

2. What does the speaker probably think is the most important piece of equipment? How do you know?

   a good tent; it is underlined

3. What will the speaker emphasize about putting out a fire? How do you know?

   putting it out safely; the word *safely* is in capital letters.

Round Decimals

Write the correct answer.

Understand → Plan → Solve → Check

1. Marion's mass is 34.4 kilograms. Round her mass to the nearest kilogram.

_____34 kilograms_____

2. Compare. Write <, > , or = in the ◯.

6.325 ⟨ > ⟩ 6.235

3. Round 87.456 to the nearest hundredth.

_____87.46_____

4. Charlene's class has 26 students. If each student makes 22 flashcards, how many cards are needed?

_____572 cards_____

Choose the letter of the correct answer.

5. Round 47.53 to the nearest tenth.

A 47.5   **C** 47.6
B 47.54   **D** 48

6. Round 6.172 and 6.091 to the nearest tenth, and compare the rounded numbers.

F 6.2 < 6.1   **H** 6.2 = 6.1
G 6.2 > 6.1   **J** 6.1 > 6.0

7. Buck collected bus fares on the Lincoln Line for 2 hours on Monday. He collected $95.50 in the first hour and $91.50 in the second hour. Then, he switched to the Andrews Line and collected $41.30 for each of the 2 hours. How much money did he collect in all?

A $259.30   **C** $274.90
B $269.60   **D** $275.16

8. Jamie collected $1,944.64 from the afternoon symphony performance and $1,986.28 from the evening symphony performance. Round each amount of money collected to the nearest hundred dollars, and compare the rounded amounts.

F $1,900.00 > $2,000.00
G $1,900.00 < $2,000.00
H $1,900.00 = $2,000.00
J $1,940.00 > $1,980.00

9. Write About It Explain how you solved Problem 8.

Possible answer: I rounded each amount to the nearest hundred dollars.

Then I compared the rounded amounts and decided which was greater.

_____

© Harcourt

Estimate Decimal Sums and Differences

Write the correct answer.

1. Estimate the sum by rounding to the nearest whole number.

$$\begin{array}{r} 2.4 \\ 1.8 \\ + 3.7 \\ \hline \end{array}$$

8

2. Estimate the difference by rounding to the nearest whole number.

$$\begin{array}{r} 6.794 \\ - 2.319 \\ \hline \end{array}$$

5

3. Order from greatest to least.

0.59   0.32   0.412

0.59; 0.412; 0.32

4. A chemist has a beaker with 14.8 liters of alcohol in it. She pours 3.9 liters of it into a container. About how much alcohol is left in the beaker?

about 11 L

Choose the letter of the correct answer.

5. Which is the most reasonable estimate of the sum?

$$\begin{array}{r} 1.72 \\ + 1.93 \\ \hline \end{array}$$

A 4   C 2
B 3   D 1

6. Which is the most reasonable estimate of the difference?

$$\begin{array}{r} 7.582 \\ - 2.816 \\ \hline \end{array}$$

F 4   H 10
G 5   J 11

7. A song is played at a fast tempo of 150 beats per minute. If the song lasts for 3 minutes 50 seconds, about how many beats are there in the song?

A about 300 beats
B about 400 beats
C about 500 beats
D about 600 beats

8. A pixel is an individual dot. Some computer monitors are 1,024 pixels wide by 768 pixels high. About how many pixels are there on such a computer screen?

F about 8,000,000
G about 800,000
H about 80,000
J about 8,000

9. Write About It Describe the steps you took to solve Problem 7.

Possible answer: I estimated 3 min 50 sec was about 4 min, then I

multiplied 150 beats × 4 min to get about 600 beats.

Add Decimals

Write the correct answer.

1. 0.8
    + 0.5

    _____ 1.3

2. 31.839
    + 40.587

    _____ 72.426

3. Natasha has a handful of pennies. She counts 28 pennies. What decimal part of a dollar does she have?

    _____ 0.28

4. Mr. Moore fills the gasoline tank in his car. He then uses $\frac{1}{4}$ of the gasoline driving to his brother's house. What fractional part of the tank of gasoline does he have left?

    _____ $\frac{3}{4}$ tank

Choose the letter of the correct answer.

5. 22.75
    + 31.35

    A 53.00 **B** 53.10 **C** 54.00 **D** 54.10

6. 0.9
    + 0.7

    F 1.6 **G** 1.16 **H** 1.06 **J** 0.16

7. A composer writes a symphony in 4 parts. Each part is twice as long as the previous part. The second part lasts for 6 minutes. How long is the entire symphony?

    A 90 min   **C** 45 min
    B 75 min   **D** 24 min

8. Mike spends $10.90 on dinner and $7.50 on a movie. He then spends $\frac{1}{2}$ of what he has left on a cab ride home. When he gets home he has $10.80 left. How much did Mike spend on the cab ride home?

    F $5.40   **H** $21.60
    G $10.80   **J** $40.00

9. **Write About It** Describe the method you used to solve Problem 7.

    Possible answer: I made a table with one column for each part; the first

    part was $\frac{1}{2}$ of 6 min, or 3 min; the third part was 6 min × 2, or 12 min;

    the fourth part was 12 min × 2, or 24 min. Then I added the times

    from each column.

Subtract Decimals

Understand ➡ Plan ➡ Solve ➡ Check

Write the correct answer.

1.   32.45
     $-$ 9.61

     22.84

2.   9.2
     $-$ 6.485

     2.715

3. Hank catches the flu, and his temperature rises to 3.2°F above normal. If normal is 98.6°F, what is Hank's temperature?

101.8°F

4. Jenny cuts 3 lengths of molding: $3\frac{3}{4}$ inches, $3\frac{3}{8}$ inches, and $3\frac{3}{16}$ inches. Which is the shortest length she cuts?

$3\frac{3}{16}$ in.

Choose the letter of the correct answer.

5.   2.4
     $-$ 1.5

   A 1.9   **B** 0.99   **C** 0.9   **D** 0.09

6.   60
     $-$ 26.82

   F 34.82   **G** 33.18   **H** 33.018   **J** 32.18

7. Long-playing vinyl records were usually meant to be played at a speed of $33\frac{1}{3}$ revolutions per minute. At this rate of speed, how many turns would a record make in 3 minutes?

   A Less than 100
   B Exactly 100
   C More than 100
   D Exactly 1,000

8. At the start of the track season, Alicia's time in the 100-meter dash was 12.25 seconds. By the end of the season, her time dropped to 11.78 seconds. Which most accurately describes how Alicia's time improved?

   F It decreased almost 0.5 sec.
   G It decreased more than 0.5 sec.
   H It decreased almost 0.75 sec.
   J It decreased more than 0.75 sec.

9. Write About It Describe the steps you took to solve Problem 7.

Possible answer: I added $33\frac{1}{3} + 33\frac{1}{3} + 33\frac{1}{3}$ so that I could compare the

sum to the answer choices; the sum was $99\frac{3}{3}$ which equals 100.

Name _____

Add and Subtract Decimals and Money

Write the correct answer.

1. 6.7
 + 3.19

_____
 9.89

2. 46.185
 − 7.2

_____
 38.985

3. Kate prices turquoise beads at four stores. She finds these prices for single beads: $0.98, $0.88, $0.95, $0.93. Order the prices from least to most expensive.

$0.88, $0.93, $0.95, $0.98

4. Victor works $5\frac{1}{4}$ hours on Friday and $7\frac{3}{4}$ hours on Saturday. How much longer does he work on Saturday than on Friday?

$2\frac{1}{2}$ hours longer

Choose the letter of the correct answer.

5. 48.4
 − 2.059

A 32.8   **C** 50.459
B 46.341   **D** 279

6. $32 − $9.85

F $9.57   **H** $22.00
G $10.00   **J** $22.15

7. Two standard settings for laser printers are 300 dots per inch (dpi) and 600 dots per inch (dpi). In a space that is one inch by one inch, the 300 dpi printer prints 300 × 300 dots. The 600 dpi printer prints 600 × 600 dots. How many dots are printed in the space by the 600 dpi printer?

A 2 times as many as the 300 dpi printer

B 3 times as many as the 300 dpi printer

C 4 times as many as the 300 dpi printer

D 5 times as many as the 300 dpi printer

8. Leanne buys a bookshelf that has the lowest shelf $3\frac{2}{4}$ in. above the floor. The next shelf up is $12\frac{3}{4}$ in. above the floor. Which book will stand up straight on the lowest shelf?

F a $9\frac{3}{4}$-in.-tall book

G a $9\frac{5}{8}$-in.-tall book

H a $9\frac{1}{2}$-in.-tall book

J a $9\frac{1}{4}$-in.-tall book

9. Write About It Describe the strategy you used to solve Problem 7.

Possible answer: I made a model on grid paper, using simpler numbers: I made a 3 by 3 square and a 6 by 6 square and compared the number of squares in them.

© Harcourt

Synthesize Information

Understand ➤ Plan ➤ Solve ➤ Check

VOCABULARY

synthesize

When a problem presents a lot of information, it is helpful to **synthesize**, or combine, the related facts. You can group the related facts in a chart. Some charts might have more than two headings. Read the following problem.

> Mr. Webb drove from his home to the airport. He drove 78.6 miles before lunch. He drove 201.7 miles after lunch. He drove 50.4 more miles. Then he realized he had missed the airport. He turned around and drove 11.6 miles back down the same road to the airport. How many miles was it from Mr. Webb's house to the airport?

1. Synthesize the information in the problem. Group the facts that are related in a chart. Complete the chart.

Numbers to Add	Numbers to Subtract
78.6	330.7
201.7	− 11.6
+ 50.4	

2. Solve the problem.

78.6 + 201.7 + 50.4 = 330.7; 330.7 − 11.6 = 319.1. It is 319.1 mi from Mr.

Webb's house to the airport.

3. Describe the strategy you used.

Possible answer: I organized the information from the problem and then

added the distances to the airport and subtracted the distance past the

airport

Synthesize the information. Show it in a chart. Solve. Check students' charts.

4. Kyra donated $2.85 to the Kids Care fund. Alex donated $7.55. May donated $5.00 less than Kyra and Alex combined. How much money did May donate? How much did the three students donate in all?

$5.40; $15.80

5. Susanna had $58.42. She spent $6.59 for a belt and $25.83 for a pair of jeans. Then she got her allowance, which was $4.50. How much money does Susanna have now?

$30.50

Explore Perimeter

Understand ➡ Plan ➡ Solve ➡ Check

Write the correct answer.

1. Find the perimeter of the figure.

16 units

2. What is the difference between 781,346 and 319,528?

461,818

3. A loaf of garlic bread is divided into 12 equal pieces. Amber and Kieren each eat two pieces. What fraction of the loaf is left?

$\frac{8}{12}$, or $\frac{2}{3}$

4. Mr. Jones buys 15 packages of hot dogs for the Outdoor Club cook out. If one package of hot dogs costs $1.65, how much does Mr. Jones spend in all?

$24.75

Choose the letter of the correct answer.

5. Keith draws a polygon that has 8 angles. Which is the correct name for the polygon?

A quadrilateral
B hexagon
C pentagon
D octagon

6. What is the perimeter of the figure?

F 2 units   H 6 units
G 4 units   J 8 units

7. Fatima sets out on an 11-mile hike at 9:15 A.M. She walks for 165 minutes and stops for 45 minutes to have lunch. At what time does she finish her lunch?

A noon   C 12:45 P.M.
B 12:15 P.M.   D 1:15 P.M.

8. The Mervin family took a 6-day vacation. Each day, they drove twice as far as they had driven the day before. If they drove 12 miles on the first day, how far did they drive during their entire vacation?

F 382 mi   H 756 mi
G 592 mi   J 1,244 mi

9. Write About It Explain how you solved Problem 1.

Possible answer: I added the lengths of the sides.

© Harcourt

Estimate and Find Perimeter

Write the correct answer.

1. Find the perimeter of the figure.

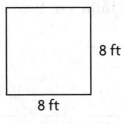

8 ft

8 ft

32 ft

2. Find the perimeter of the figure.

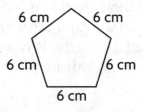

6 cm   6 cm

6 cm   6 cm

6 cm

30 cm

3. The perimeter of a rectangle is 42 inches. The length is 12 inches. What is the width?

9 inches

4. Write the product of the number of sides of a triangle, a quadrilateral, a pentagon, a hexagon, and an octagon.

2,880

Choose the letter of the correct answer.

5. Which of these has a remainder of 2?

A 70 ÷ 8   C 55 ÷ 6
B 65 ÷ 9   D 48 ÷ 7

6. Which name best describes the lines formed by the two rails on a straight stretch of railroad track?

F perpendicular   H intersecting
G parallel   J obtuse

7. Gina puts on a CD at 7:35 P.M. She plays one half of the CD, then pauses the player at 8:10 P.M. How many minutes of music are there on the CD?

A 35 min   C 70 min
B 60 min   D 75 min

8. Steven's living room is L-shaped. He measures four of the walls. They measure 12 ft, 14 ft, 14 ft, and 12 ft. The perimeter of the room is 104 ft. If the last two walls have the same length, what is the length of each?

F 52 ft   H 22 ft
G 26 ft   J 20 ft

9. **Write About It** Describe the method you used to solve Problem 8.

Possible answer: I added the lengths of the 4 measured walls, then I

subtracted that sum from the total perimeter: 104 − 52 = 52; I divided the

difference by 2.

Name _____

Circumference

Write the correct answer.

Understand ➡ Plan ➡ Solve ➡ Check

1. A triangle has a perimeter of 49 yards. One side has a length of 21 yards and another side has a length of 10 yards. What is the length of the third side?

18 yd

2. Estimate the circumference of a circle with a radius of 9 cm.

about 54 cm

3. 3,257
   × 45

146,565

4. Estimate the circumference of the circle shown at the right.

12 mi

about 36 mi

Choose the letter of the correct answer.

5. Which of the solids below has a triangular face?

   A cube
   B rectangular prism
   C cylinder
   D triangular pyramid

6. Estimate the diameter of a circle whose circumference is about 12 meters long.

   F about 1 m   H about 4 m
   G about 2 m   J about 6 m

7. What is the perimeter of a rectangle with a length of 26 inches and a width of 14 inches?

   A 82 in.
   B 80 in.
   C 78 in.
   D 76 in.

8. Estimate the circumference of a circle whose diameter is 256 centimeters long.

   F 798 cm
   G 792 cm
   H 791 cm
   J 768 cm

9. **Write About It** How did you find the circumference in Problem 2?

Possible answer: Since the radius is half the diameter, I multiplied the

radius by 2 and then multiplied this number by 3. This gave an estimate

of the circumference.

Analyzing Information

Understand ➤ Plan ➤ Solve ➤ Check

When you decide whether information is important or unimportant when solving a problem, you are **analyzing** the information. Ask yourself whether the information helps you to answer the question. Underline the important information.

VOCABULARY
analyze

The school playground holds about 50 children. The playground is shaped like a triangle and has a perimeter of 211 feet. Two sides of the playground are each 48 feet long. How long is the third side of the playground?

1. Analyze the information. Label the information as important or unimportant and explain why in the chart below.

Information	Explanation
The school playground holds about 50 children.	Possible answer: Unimportant. You don't need the information to find the length of the third side.
The playground is shaped like a triangle and has a perimeter of 211 feet.	Possible answer: Important. You can draw a triangle to help solve the problem. Use the formula for the perimeter of a triangle to help solve.
Two sides of the playground are each 48 feet long.	Possible answer: Important. Label the diagram and use the formula to find the length of the missing side.

2. Solve the problem. ____The third side of the playground is 115 feet long.____

3. Describe the problem solving strategy you used. ____Possible answer: I used a formula to solve the problem.____

Underline the important information. Use a formula to solve.

4. Ms. Sing's students want to plant vegetables. The triangular-shaped garden has a perimeter of 108 feet. One side of the garden is 43 feet long and another side is 29 feet long. How long is the third side of the garden?

_____36 ft_____

5. Sally runs 4 miles every other day. She has run on 2 parts of a triangular-shaped path that are 0.45 mile and 0.58 mile long. The perimeter of the path is 1.5 miles. How much farther does Sally have to jog to complete the path?

_____0.47 mi_____

Estimate Area

Write the correct answer.

1. Estimate the area of the figure. Each square is 1 sq in.

Possible estimate: 6 sq in.

2. The diagram shows a pond. Estimate the area of the pond. Each square is 1 square yard.

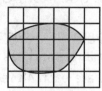

Possible estimate: 12.5 sq yd

3. A pizza is divided into 8 equal pieces. Clark and Karen each eat three slices of the pizza. What fraction of the pizza is left?

$\frac{2}{8}$, or $\frac{1}{4}$

4. Mr. Grieg puts 14 gallons of gas in his car. If the gas costs $1.85 per gallon, how much does Mr. Grieg spend in all?

$25.90

Choose the letter of the correct answer.

5. Which decimal is equivalent to $1\frac{4}{100}$?

A 1.4   C 1.44
B 1.04   D 1.004

6. Morris buys one 10-pound bag of flour. He uses 5 ounces of the flour. How much flour is left?

F 5 ounces   **H** 155 ounces
G 45 ounces   J 160 ounces

7. Which is the best estimate of the area of the figure? Each square is 1 sq cm.

A 5.5 sq cm   **C** 10.5 sq cm
B 8 sq cm   D 13 sq cm

8. Ms. Folinaro drew a plan of her garden on grid paper. Each square represents 1 square foot. Which is the best estimate of the area of her garden?

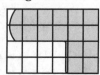

F 10 sq ft   H 20 sq ft
G 15 sq ft   J 24 sq ft

9. Write About It Explain how you found your answer to Problem 8?

Possible answer: I counted the number of whole squares and almost-full squares. Then I added to estimate the area.

Name _____

Find Area

Understand ➡ Plan ➡ Solve ➡ Check

Write the correct answer.

1. Write the area of the rectangle.

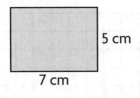

7 cm, 5 cm

_____ 35 sq cm _____

2. Write the area of the rectangle.

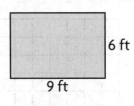

9 ft, 6 ft

_____ 54 sq ft _____

3. What is the perimeter of a garden that has sides that measure 36 ft, 18 ft, 28 ft, 19 ft, and 17 ft?

_____ 118 ft _____

4. Name the solid figure that has one square face and four triangular faces.

_____ square pyramid _____

Choose the letter of the correct answer.

5. Which plane figure has more than six angles?

A quadrilateral
B pentagon
C hexagon
D octagon

6. The perimeter of a square is 24 feet. What is its area?

F 12 sq ft
G 24 sq ft
H 36 sq ft
J 48 sq ft

7. Rhonda drew this diagram of her kitchen. What is the area of the kitchen floor?

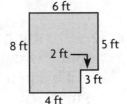

6 ft
8 ft 2 ft 5 ft
3 ft
4 ft

A 24 sq ft
B 30 sq ft
C 42 sq ft
D 48 sq ft

8. How many four-digit numbers can you make using the digits 1, 2, 3, and 4 without repeating any of the digits in the same number?

F 10 numbers
G 12 numbers
H 24 numbers
J 28 numbers

9. Write About It Explain how you found the area in Problem 7.

Possible answer: First, I divided the figure into 2 rectangles. One rectangle is 6 ft × 5 ft. The other rectangle is 3 ft × 4 ft. I found the area of

each rectangle and added to find the total area.

© Harcourt

Name _____

Relate Area and Perimeter

Understand ➡ Plan ➡ Solve ➡ Check

Write the correct answer.

1. Write the perimeter and the area of the figure.

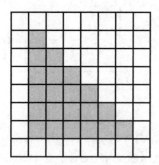

   24 units; 21 sq units
   _____

2. Which two figures have the same area but different perimeters?

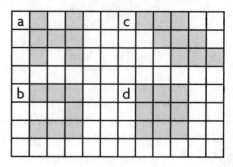

   c and d
   _____

3. Nadia's parents are carpeting their family room. The room is a rectangle that measures 6 yards by 5 yards. How many square yards of carpeting do they need?

   _30 sq yd_
   _____

4. Pete walks to the intersection of two roads. He notices that the corner he is standing on is a right angle. What type of intersecting lines do the roads form?

   perpendicular lines
   _____

Choose the letter of the correct answer.

5. Which of these letters is **not** formed entirely of line segments?

   A A   B X   C Y   **D** R

6. Which figure is **not** a polygon?

   F triangle   H hexagon
   G square   **J** circle

7. The area of a rectangle is 36 sq in. Which of these is **not** a possible perimeter?

   A 40 in.   C 26 in.
   B 36 in.   D 18 in.

8. Les is cutting polygons out of paper. He cuts the four corners off of a square. What polygon did he make?

   F pentagon   H hexagon
   G octagon   J triangle

9. **Write About It** What strategy did you use to solve Problem 8? Explain.

   Possible answer: I acted the problem out by cutting out a square and then

   cutting the four corners off of it.

© Harcourt

Compare and Contrast

Understand ➡ Plan ➡ Solve ➡ Check

Sometimes it is helpful to compare and contrast information when you are solving a problem. When you compare and contrast, you identify ways that items are alike and ways they are different.

Read the following problem.

Janine has cut different size pieces of fabric to make pillowcases. The second piece of fabric in each pair is larger than the first. She wants to know how the perimeters are related. How do the perimeters change?

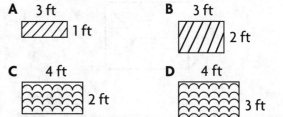

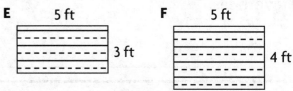

1. Compare and contrast each pair of fabrics. Complete the chart.

Fabric	Alike	Different
A and B	They have the same length.	Width of B is 1 more than width of A. Perimeters are 8 ft and 10 ft.
C and D	They have the same length.	Width of D is 1 more than width of C. Perimeters are 12 ft and 14 ft.
E and F	They have the same length.	Width of F is 1 more than width of E. Perimeters are 16 ft and 18 ft.

2. Solve the problem. Each time the width is increased by 1 foot, the perimeter is increased by 2 feet.

Use a chart to compare and contrast the perimeters in each problem. Solve.

Check students' charts.

3. Table A has a length of 6 feet and a width of 4 feet. Table B is 2 feet longer and 2 feet wider. How does the increase in length and width affect the perimeter?

The perimeter is increased

by 8 feet.

4. Picture A has a length of 8 feet and a width of 4 feet. Picture B is half as wide and half as long. How does the decrease in length and width affect the perimeter?

The perimeter is decreased

by half.

© Harcourt

Faces, Edges, and Vertices

Understand ➡ Plan ➡ Solve ➡ Check

Write the correct answer.

1. Write the names of the plane figures that are faces of the solid figure.

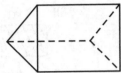

rectangles and triangles

2. What solid figure can you see in the drawing?

cylinder

3. Name a solid figure that has 8 vertices.

cube or rectangular prism

4. Write the names of the faces and the number of each kind of face on a triangular pyramid.

4 triangles

Choose the letter of the correct answer.

5. Which figure has the fewest faces?

  A cube
  B triangular pyramid
  C rectangular prism
  D square pyramid

6. Neal challenges Lynn to name a solid figure that has no edges. Lynn names one. Which figure does she name?

  F cube
  G triangular prism
  H square pyramid
  J sphere

7. A football team wins a national championship and 43,180 people are expected to attend the celebration. The arena holds only 22,520 people. About how many people will have to be turned away?

  A about 32,000   C about 18,000
  B about 20,000   D about 11,000

8. Karen decorated picture frames. She put 6 flowers on each of 5 frames. She put 4 flowers on each of 3 frames. How many flowers did she use?

  F 42   H 29
  G 35   J 18

9. **Write About It** Explain how you solved Problem 7.

Possible answer: I rounded first and then estimated:

43,000 − 23,000 = 20,000.

Patterns for Solid Figures

Understand ➡ **Plan** ➡ **Solve** ➡ **Check**

Write the correct answer.

1. What solid figure model does the net below make?

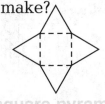

square pyramid

2. Valerie needs to estimate the cost of her bill. Her bill includes $3.56, $1.35, $3.67, and $7.15. Round each price to the nearest dollar, then add.

$16.00

3. How many squares will the net of this solid figure have?

six squares

4. What fraction of the circle is shaded in the picture shown?

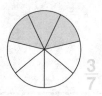

$\frac{3}{7}$

Choose the letter of the correct answer.

5. What solid figure model does this net make?

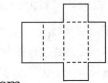

A cube
B rectangular prism
C cone
D square pyramid

6. What solid figure does this net make?

F triangular prism
G triangular pyramid
H cube
J cylinder

7. What is the perimeter of the figure below?

A 35 cm
B 31 cm
C 28 cm
D 27 cm

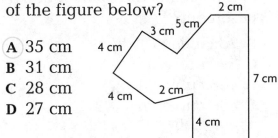

8. What is the area of the shaded figure below?

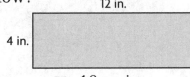

12 in.

4 in.

F 48 sq in. **H** 16 sq in.
G 32 sq in. **J** 9 sq in.

9. Write About It How did you find the area in Problem 8?

Possible answer: I used the formula for area, A = l × w and replaced the values for length and width in the formula. Then I multiplied. A = 12 × 4; A = 48 sq. in.

Name _____

Estimate and Find Volume of Prisms

Write the correct answer.

1. What is the volume of the solid figure shown below?

_____48 cubic units_____

2. What is the volume of the cube shown below?

_____125 cubic units_____

3. 683
   × 23
   _____
   15,709

4. The area of a rectangle is 432 square meters and the width is 9 meters. What is the length of the rectangle?

_____48 meters_____

Choose the letter of the correct answer.

5. The sum of the number of faces, edges, and vertices on a figure is 14. What is the figure?

   A rectangular prism
   B triangular prism
   C triangular pyramid
   D square pyramid

6. George has a box that is 3 feet wide, 4 feet long, and 1 foot high. What is the volume of his box?

   F 12 cubic feet
   G 12 square feet
   H 8 cubic feet
   J 4 square feet

7. Find the length of the unknown side if the perimeter of the triangle below is 56 meters.

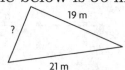

   A 14 m   C 35 m
   B 16 m   D 96 m

8. Jamie's basement is 13 yards long, 12 yards wide, and 3 yards high. What is the volume of her basement?

   F 28 cubic yd
   G 39 cubic yd
   H 468 cubic yd
   J 486 cubic yd

9. **Write About It** Explain how you solved Problem 5.

Possible answer: I found the sum for each

of the solids listed until I found 14.

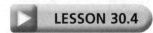

Choose Relevant Information

Sometimes a word problem contains information that may *not* help you solve the problem. You must decide which information is **relevant**, or needed to solve the problem. Read the following problem.

> Antonia is going to travel 2,500 miles. She will be gone 10 days. She has a suitcase that is 36 inches long, 18 inches wide, and 20 inches deep. What is the volume of her suitcase?

1. Read each fact from the problem. Write whether the fact is *relevant* or *not relevant* to solve the problem.

   a. Antonia is going to travel 2,500 miles.

   _____ not relevant _____

   b. Antonia will be gone 10 days.

   _____ not relevant _____

   c. She has a suitcase that is 36 inches long, 18 inches wide, and 20 inches deep.

   _____ relevant _____

2. Solve the problem.

   _____ 36 × 18 × 20 = 12,960 cubic inches _____

3. Describe the strategy you used.

   _____ Possible answer: I found the volume of the suitcase _____

   _____ using only the dimensions of the suitcase. _____

Draw a line through the information that is not relevant. Solve.

4. Lauren dug a hole that was 4 feet deep, 5 feet wide, and 6 feet long. She buried a box in that hole. The box was 2 feet by 2 feet by 3 feet. What was the volume of the box Lauren buried?

   _____ 12 cubic feet _____

5. Rocky has a box that has a volume of 36 cubic inches. The width of the box is 4 inches. The height of the box is 3 inches. He has 3 crickets and one 7-inch snake in his box. What is the length of the box?

   _____ 3 inches _____